Me diterranean

Compiled and edited by Tom Le Bas
and Clare Peel
Cover photograph by Corrie Wingate
Series Editor: Tony Halliday

Berlitz POCKET GUIDE

Ports of Call
Mediterranean

First Edition 2005

NO part of this book may be reproduced, stored in a retrieval system or transmitted in any form or means electronic, mechanical, photocopying, recording or otherwise, without prior written permission from Berlitz Publishing. Brief text quotations with use of photographs are exempted for book review purposes only.

PHOTOGRAPHY

Kurt Ammann 130; Pete Bennett 71, 73, 89, 90, 91, 92, 93, 140, 142, 143, 145, 159, 160, 161, 162, 176, 179, 180, 181, 187, 188, 189, 191, 199, 201, 226, 228; Berlitz 59, 217; Elizabeth Boleman-Herring 10, 170, 171; Chris Bradley 223; Conor Caffrey 15; Chris Coe 25, 27, 33, 36, 65, 119, 120, 121, 123, 127, 131, 132, 133, 137; Jon Davison 74, 126; Jerry Dennis 9, 34, 35, 39, 41, 67, 102, 103, 104; Guglielmo Galvin 109; Glyn Genin 30, 48, 52, 95, 122, 125, 139, 141, 144, 183, 184/5; Chris Godet 129; Frances Gransden 110; Mike Griffiths 56, 58; Tony Halliday 14, 193, 194, 195, 197, 198; Britta Jaschinski 51; Axel Krause 224, 227; Ros Miller 12; Anna Mockford and Nick Bonnetti 7, 172, 173, 175; Paul Murphy 204, 205; Gary John Norman 11, 57, 61, 64, 214; P&O Cruises 18; Sarah Louise Ramsey 15; Mark Read 16, 17, 45, 47, 68, 96, 97, 98, 99, 100, 150; Neil Schlecht 21, 29, 42, 43, 46, 50; Gordon Singer 55; George Taylor 203, 206; George Taylor and Guglielmo Galvin 105, 107; Turismo de Lisboa 76; V&A Picture Library 8; Bill Wassman 53, 54, 76, 77, 79, 81, 83, 84/5, 87, 111, 112, 158; Phil Wood 13, 31, 114, 115, 116, 117, 208, 210, 211, 212; Gregory Wrona 62, 63, 128, 147, 149, 152, 153, 155, 157, 164, 167, 177, 178, 190, 216, 218, 220.

CONTACTING THE EDITORS

Every effort has been made to provide accurate information in this publication, but changes are inevitable. The publisher cannot be responsible for any resulting loss, inconvenience or injury. We would appreciate it if readers would call our attention to any errors or outdated information by contacting Berlitz Publishing, PO Box 7910, London SE1 1WE, England.
Fax: (44) 20 7403 0290.
Email: berlitz@apaguide.co.uk.

All Rights Reserved
© *2005 Apa Publications GmbH & Co.
Verlag KG, Singapore Branch, Singapore
Printed in Singapore by Insight Print
Services (Pte) Ltd, 38 Joo Koon Road,
Singapore 628990. Tel: (65) 6865-1600.
Fax: (65) 6861-6438
Berlitz Trademark Reg. U.S. Patent Office
and other countries. Marca Registrada*

Turquoise seas against a white-washed village church: the Greek islands at their most captivating (page 168)

The strange and colourful legacy of Gaudí sets the tone for a visit to stylish Barcelona (page 42), Spain's second city

Enigmatic and eternal, the pyramids (page 227) continue to cast a spell over visitors to Egypt

TOP TEN ATTRACTIONS

he colossal
plosseum
age 113)
hets the
ppetite for
e treasures
Rome ▼

Of all the Classical sites that
evoke the glories of ancient
Greece, Athens' Parthenon
(page 159) is paramount

Arab souks and Roman remains
are among the alluring mix of
attractions in Tunisia (page 214) ➤

The stunning
Alhambra (page
35) is the focal
point of Spain's
city of Granada

Two great
mpires left a
asting legacy
in Istanbul
(page 193)
➤

Sun, sea and sand form a vivid
backdrop to the French Riviera
(page 77) ▼

For sheer beauty and
elegance, Venice (page
120) has no equal ▼

CONTENTS

CRUISING THE MEDITERRANEAN

Douglas Ward, author of the annual Berlitz Cruising &
Cruise Ships, *which surveys more than 250 cruise ships
in detail, reports on the growing appeal of holidays afloat*

'To dream and dream…', wrote Homer in *The Iliad*, a
poem set in the Mediterranean region. Those dreams
have remained a potent siren call for travellers through the
centuries. When, in 1844, P&O offered the 33-year-old
writer William Makepeace Thackeray a voyage to the eastern Mediterranean in return for publicity favours, he jumped
at the opportunity, and in the resulting *Notes of a Journey
from Cornhill to Cairo* he reported that, when the ship
entered the Bay of Gibraltar, the water looked bluer than
anything he had ever seen, 'except for Miss Smith's eyes'.

By the 1920s, cruising to the Mediterranean had become
almost commonplace, with sailings from Britain of at least
three weeks' duration. In 1961, an important milestone was
reached when Epirotiki Lines introduced fly-cruising, taking
the bold step of arranging flights, a cruise and transport to
and from the port, all wrapped neatly in a package that could
also include overnight hotel accommodation for those wishing to extend their stay. Today more than 50 cruise companies and tour operators offer ocean-going Mediterranean
cruises of between three and 30 days, using approximately
100 vessels. May to October is the standard cruise season,
although some operators start as early as March and continue
as late as November.

Some port authorities, strangled by official bureaucracy,
have been slow to respond to the steady growth in cruising,
scarcely distinguishing between cruise ships and ferries and
assuming that all cruise passengers want the same holiday
experience. Some ports (Athens, Barcelona, Cannes, Nice,
Portofino and Venice, for example) suffer from congestion.

However, as the industry grows, improvements are taking place. Passenger facilities are being improved, as terminals are enhanced or newly built, and exciting new cruise ports are being added to itineraries. This all reflects the growth in cruise passengers worldwide and to the Mediterranean in particular. In recent years, the Mediterranean has become firmly established as the most popular cruise destination after the Caribbean. From the UK, though, it

Taking a dip in clear blue waters, Zákynthos, Greece

remains the number one choice. Cruising's popularity is set to expand further, with companies wooing not only North Americans and Europeans en masse but also, increasingly, catering to individual nationalities. Some companies target entire families, from grandparents to grandchildren, while others operate child-free ships.

Although no single cruise covers every port, cruise ships do offer a comfortable way of exploring the area's rich mix of cultures, history, traditions, architecture, lifestyles and cuisines. For some, the appeal is mainly the educational experience of sampling unfamiliar cultures. For others, it is the chance to have a safe, crime-free holiday – something that cannot always be guaranteed on land. And, for romantics, it is a chance to fulfil their ambition of sailing the Mediterranean's azure waters in the wake of Homer and Thackeray. The cruise industry is, after all, in the business of selling dreams.

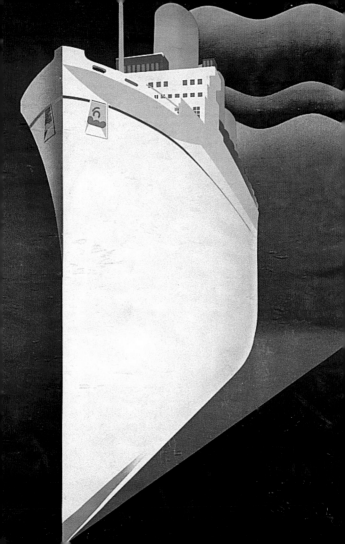

INTRODUCTION

For many people, the Mediterranean epitomises the warm, southern good life. The tang of citrus in the sunlit air; a terrace overlooking endless olive groves and vineyards; a frescoed church over the next hill, just beyond the Classical ruins; cobbled streets leading to whitewashed walls and a secluded inn studded with hand-painted tiles; a patrician villa with terracotta rooftops owned by an amiably impoverished count; pastel-coloured yachts bobbing gently in the harbour. The dream may include a flamenco night, a harvest festival or a muezzin's call to prayer.

The pleasure and advantage of a cruise is that you don't have to settle for an idealised image of the Mediterranean. Instead, a procession of evocative ports unfurls to suit every mood, exposing a kaleidoscope of cultures, from gondolas swishing down the Grand Canal in Venice to ferry boats on the Bosphorus, past mosques and minarets.

A Mediterranean voyage invites you to ponder on ruined civilisations and the heritage of ancient cultures. But it also serves up such vibrant cities as Barcelona and Nice, with the taste of every new culture matched by the local cuisine. In terms of diversity, the Mediterranean represents what is probably the world's greatest cultural spread of any comparable geographical area. The sea laps the shores of Christendom and Islam, Europe, Asia and Africa.

Opposite: majestic art deco liner. Right: Florentine dome

Preserving Identity

Countries bordering the Mediterranean have weathered invasions and intermingling for over 5,000 years. Scrape the surface of every seemingly unique nation state and you unearth traces of myriad civilisations underneath; any new building project inevitably reveals Roman foundations or Classical columns. Yet the miracle is that each country remains obdurately itself. Despite wars and vicissitudes, little has diluted national pride, or even island identity. Corsicans pride themselves on their divergence from France while Sardinians claim that allegiance to Italy is only a small part of their identity. As for the Greek Islands, the residents of Rhodes, Crete and Corfu delight in their Greek spirit and Classical heritage, but it is a racial pride nurtured by a glorification of their own island history, whether Crusader, Minoan or Venetian.

Chapel of Ágios Arsénos, Corfu

Despite the intermingling down the centuries, the result is not the proverbial melting pot, a lumpen stew of similar peoples, but models of diversity. This is as true of tiny outposts such as Malta and Gibraltar as it is of countries as significant as Spain, Italy, Greece and Turkey.

Wars & Their Aftermath

War and invasions have helped to determine the fate and character of the Mediterranean lands. Leaving aside the battles of antiquity, there have also been wars between civilisations and faiths. The Crusades were initiated by European Christendom between the 11th and 14th centuries to recover the Holy Land from the Muslims. The First Crusade (1095–99) led to the capture of Antioch and Jerusalem but the ensuing massacre of Muslims and Jews provoked retribution from the Arab world.

Tinerfeña, from Tenerife

The impact of the Crusades was substantial. Many who followed in the wake of the pilgrims and Crusaders created commercial links, or even settled on the shores of the Mediterranean. They also gave rise to the great military orders, from the Knights Templar to the Knights of St John, who built churches and castles.

Disputes, Trade, Culture

Some places in the Mediterranean, such as Cyprus and Gibraltar, still have disputed national allegiances. On a far greater scale, the conflict between Israel and Palestine over the latter's desire for statehood remains a matter of bloody dispute. Yet trade, even more than war, has shaped the civilisations of the Mediterranean world, spawning artistic cross-fertilisation and cultural links.

From literature to geometry, mechanics and hydrostatics, cultures borrowed from one another, and nothing represents the flowers of cross-cultural pollination more than art and architecture. Norman Gothic architecture in southern

Venice was once the heart of a powerful trading empire

Europe was subverted by Moorish models, and Arabs were preceded by the Greeks, Romans and Byzantines who planted their architectural models on Mediterranean shores. Byzantine goldsmiths, craftsmen and iconographers left shimmering mosaics in countless basilicas.

The greatest Mediterranean trading empires of Genoa, Pisa, Venice and Barcelona spanned the Mediterranean, enriching the cultural fabric of the home cities with a mix of Byzantine, Moorish, Norman and Spanish models. Yet much comes back to the Greek contribution and the spread of Hellenistic culture: the temple of Artemis (Diana) at Ephesus in modern-day Turkey was one of the seven wonders of the ancient world, a Greek city founded in the 4th century BC.

Cradle of Civilisation

Egypt's gift to history was the pyramids, but, as the cradle of Classical civilisation, Greece has left a much greater legacy in the fields of mythology, mathematics, science, architecture, sculpture, philosophy and politics, and the dawn of democracy. Architecture reached its greatest glory during the Classical period, when the Parthenon was built. Its perfect symmetry remains an eternal anchor in the hectic lives of proud Athenians.

During the ensuing Hellenistic period, from the death of Alexander the Great in 323BC until the accession of the

Roman Emperor Augustus in 27BC, the Greek way of life colonised the Mediterranean.

A Voyage Through Time

Classical culture reorientated itself further west, as Roman civilisation followed Greek decline. Much of Mediterranean culture resonates to the chords of cultural one-upmanship between these heavyweight civilisations. Not that they were ever polar opposites: the Roman model, from its Greek-inspired mythology to Hellenistic-inspired architecture, was heavily dependent upon the Greek Classical model. Southern Italy has Greek ruins that often surpass those in Greece. Even the much-lauded Italian Renaissance, a thousand years later, looked to the glories of ancient Greece for its inspiration in everything from philosophy and first principles to literature, learning and the arts.

Byzantine mosaic, Híos

The Mediterranean shores are dotted with Roman remains, from Carthage in Tunisia to Baalbek in the Lebanon. The legacy of the Roman Empire was the Latin language, a universally accepted calendar and a coherent body of law that still underpins the Continental legal system. Another lasting legacy was Christianity and the institution of the papacy in Rome.

Aya Sofya, Istanbul

The Mysterious East

Istanbul owes its origins to both the Greeks and the Romans. Founded by the Greeks in about 676BC as Byzantion, it was renamed Byzantium by the Romans; under Constantine, the first Christian emperor, it became Constantinople, capital of the Eastern Roman (Byzantine) Empire that lasted until the Ottoman conquest in 1453. The Ottoman Empire's reach was unrivalled, with Constantinople cast as the administrative centre of the sprawling eastern Mediterranean world. It lasted six centuries, albeit with a long period of decline, coming formally to an end only in 1922, when Turkey was declared a republic.

While the dream of the Sultan and his court lasted, it provided inspiration for *A Thousand and One Nights* fantasies and fuelled the myth of the exoticism of the East. No topic caught the European male imagination more than the tales of bevies of beautiful concubines held in harems purely for the delight of one master, the Sultan. As a secret world of the senses, the harem and the symbolism of its lovely songbirds imprisoned in a gilded cage, has lost little of its allure.

African Links

As for cruising Egypt, Lebanon, Morocco, Tunisia and Palestine, these lands have been termed the wilder shores of the Mediterranean, the Levant ('where the sun rises'), the biblical lands. The Egyptians were indeed the first recorded people to sail the Mediterranean, on modified river boats propelled by punt-shaped hulls and single sails. Alexandria might have lost its lustre, but from the port you can visit the pyramids of Giza, one of the surviving wonders of the world. In Lebanon, Baalbek is among the best-preserved Classical ruins in the Middle East, while Byblos is a precious, ancient city.

Along with Tangier in Morocco, Tunis is the most popular port of call in North Africa, with visits to the ruined Phoenician city of Carthage, recolonised by the Romans. Given the indecipherability of the Roman ruins, it makes sense to call in at the superb Bardo Museum in Tunis, which has some of the finest Roman mosaics in the world, salvaged from different North African sites, and ranging from portraits to myths and maritime scenes. The new kid on the block in terms of tourism is Libya, welcomed into the international fold now that Gadaffi has renounced his old ways, and fascinating in that its doors have only just opened to tourism.

**Solid-gold funeral masks,
Egyptian Museum, Cairo**

If any country can lay claim to having deep cultural links across the Mediterranean to Africa, it is Spain. Early in the 8th century, Spain succumbed to the Moorish conquest, with little resistance from its Celtic-Iberian inhabitants. In its 8th-century heyday, Córdoba was one of the most enlightened and cultured cities in the Mediterranean world. The Moorish Golden Age came to an end in 1492, however, when the last dynasty took flight to North Africa. Even so, Toledo, Granada, Seville and Cádiz all flourished in Moorish Spain, and the interplay with Christian culture means that some of the greatest churches were at one time mosques.

As for palaces, Granada's Alhambra is the apogee of Moorish architecture in Spain, if not the entire Mediterranean. Seville's Holy Week processions, meanwhile, manages to encapsulate the emotional fever pitch of a Mediterranean Christian festival and the Moorish passion beyond. Hooded devotees escort sacred images to the ear-splitting sound of a funeral march. In Cádiz, one of Europe's oldest continuously inhabited cities, the riotous pre-Lenten carnival provides an even clearer link with pagan antiquity.

The Alhambra's exquisite Patio de Arrayanes, southern Spain

As a popular cruising destination, Spain's ports of call provide access to Andalusian Seville (via Cádiz), to the Moorish Alhambra in Granada (via Málaga) and to Mallorca, via Palma, the island's capital. Barcelona, closer to the French border, differs from most other Spanish ports of call by being resolutely European in temperament and design. As well as being the capital of Catalunya, Barcelona considers itself on a par with the grandest European cities, and is one of the liveliest ports of call. From Europe's most bizarre church (the unfinished Sagrada Família) to streets lined with talented buskers, enticing tapas bars and designer boutiques, Barcelona oozes exuberance from every street corner.

A glass of Croatian red

Mediterranean Food

The Mediterranean diet is frequently celebrated as one of the world's healthiest. For most Westerners, it represents archetypal comfort food, full of robust flavours and fresh, wholesome ingredients. The delicious combination of local food and drink, including red wine, is linked to longevity, a healthy heart and a low incidence of cancer. The Mediterranean diet is a recipe for health, being rich in vegetables, olives, virgin olive oil, garlic, honey, wine, ripe tomatoes, pasta, rice, fish and citrus fruits.

Whether eating out in Barcelona or Bodrum, Taormina or Tunis, diners face an array of common foods, albeit served in a bewildering variety of ways. In short, a meal served in an old-time Greek taverna, a family-run Italian trattoria or a frenetic Lebanese *mezze* den should still include some of the classic Mediterranean staples – such as bread drizzled in olive oil, grilled sardines served with ripe tomatoes, or tiny squid blistering on a charcoal grill – that are a delight for jaded palettes.

WHERE TO GO

Mediterranean cruises cover a wide area and a huge range of destinations, from the bustling Catalan capital, Barcelona, to chic Riviera harbours, historic Italian cities, tranquil Greek islands and vibrant North African ports. Once you have decided on the kind of ship on which you wish to travel and the broad itinerary that suits your taste, time and budget, the next step is to look in more detail at the destinations you will be visiting.

This section, arranged by country, is intended to help you with this. We include a selection of ports for each country, some of which are home ports, some of which feature on most itineraries that visit a particular area, and others that are ports of call only for small ships or those on specialised cruises.

> To get the most from shore excursions, read up on them beforehand. Don't overbook excursions – a full schedule can be punishing on the pocket as well as physically exhausting.

Some ports are visited chiefly because they give access to towns or sites of great beauty or historical or architectural interest, in which case those destinations receive more attention here than the ports of call themselves. All the cruise lines run shore excursions to these places, but we give advice here on how to make these same trips independently.

Note that unexpected changes of schedule can occur when cruising, due to bad weather or other causes, and a much-anticipated destination may be missed out. Barring that eventuality, all you have to do is let your floating hotel carry you on your way.

Cruise liner in the harbour at Villefranche-sur-Mer, France

Portugal

Climate Spring and summer are the best times of year to visit. The weather starts getting warm in May and June and usually stays warm to very hot until September. Apart from the Algarve, nights can be cool even in summer. Summers are generally hot throughout the country with endless days of sunshine.

Time zone GMT (summer time GMT+1).

Opening Times On Sundays and saints' days, most shops are shut. On other days, some stores close for two or three hours at lunchtime.

What to Buy Look out for laceware and rugs, pottery and ceramics, straw bags and bottles of port wine, sherry or *vinho verde.*

Money Matters Euro.

Public Holidays 1 January, Good Friday, 25 April, 1 May, Corpus Christi (early June), 10 June, 15 August, 5 October, 1 Nov, 1, 8, 25 December.

Etiquette The Portuguese are usually very courteous and hospitable. For some reason, stretching in public is considered rude.

Tipping Restaurant bills usually include service, but a small tip may be added for excellent service. Around 10 percent is usual for taxis.

Hazards and Security Portugal in general is a safe country. Major tourist areas such as the Algarve experience more petty crime than other parts of Portugal, though crimes involving violence against tourists are rare. Report any theft to the nearest police station or local tourist office. You must report any losses to the local police within 24 hours and obtain a copy of your statement for insurance purposes. Lisbon is infamous for pickpockets, particularly on the metro and Rossio square. You are advised not to walk in the Bairro Alto or Alfama areas at night unless in a group.

Drugs and Medicines Portuguese pharmacies, or *farmacias*, display a green cross on a white background outside or within the store window. Generally, the pharmacies in Portugal are reliable.

Emergency Telephone Numbers All emergencies 112; fire 60 60 60; ambulance (Red Cross) 301 77 77.

Traditional Portuguese *azulejos*, hand-painted, glazed, ceramic tiles

PORTUGAL

Portugal's past as a great seafaring nation makes its principal port and capital an obvious choice for many cruises. The approach to Lisbon up the River Tagus (Tejo in Portuguese) is the dramatic prelude to a city full of reminders of its maritime history. Also on the cruising map are the country's second city, elegant Porto, and to the south, in the Algarve, Portimão. The final part of the chapter deals with the group of Atlantic islands discovered by the Portuguese in 1419 and which is often included on Mediterranean cruise itineraries – Madeira.

Lisbon

Although it was put on the world map by 15th-century marine explorers such as Vasco da Gama who used it as a base for expeditions to Africa and India, **Lisbon** (Lisboa)

lacks the immediately recognisable icons of most other European capitals. However, it has its own relaxed charm and fewer crowds than most capitals (there are only 700,000 residents), and is hence easy to navigate. There is a clearly defined centre (Baixa) within easy reach of the two districts that visitors usually want to see (Bairro Alto and Alfama). Lisbon is also within easy range of the sophisticated coastal resorts of Cascais and Estoril, with the historic hill-top village of Sintra – Byron's 'Eden' – not much further away.

Although early-morning mist sometimes obscures the views, it is always an engaging 15km (10-mile) journey along the River Tagus, past the Belém and the distinctive Monument to the Discoveries with its statue of Henry the Navigator and a host of famous explorers jutting out into the river. Then, after passing below Europe's longest suspension bridge, your ship docks at the main port (Doca de Alcântara),

The view across Lisbon from the Tagus

which is approximately 5km (3 miles) from the centre of the city.

Cruise lines usually organise a shuttle bus to ferry passengers between the port and Praça do Comercio, the main square by the waterfront. It's easy to get into the city centre independently too. One option is to travel in old-world style on the historic wooden trams. No. 15, from the centre to Belém and No. 28 to Alfama are the most picturesque routes.

> The Bairro Alto is the most popular place for eating out in the evening; typical little local restaurants are called *tascas*. There are also lively restaurants on the waterfront docks, the Doca de Santo Amaro. Fish is a speciality; dishes include *arroz de marisco*, a delicious rice-and-shellfish dish, and a splendid fish stew, *caldeirada de peixe*.

City Centre

The city centre, where most of the many points of interest are to be found, is divided into three districts – Baixa, Bairro Alto and Alfama.

Baixa is a predominantly 18th- to 19th-century district with a rectangular grid system, created after the 1755 earthquake levelled the old city. It stretches across the flat area flanked by the steep hills of Alfama to the east and Bairro Alto to the west, extending from Praça do Comércio, a large pedestrianised square bordered by pink arcaded buildings, through a triumphal arch over Rua Augusta and past the city's principal shopping area, banks, cafés and restaurants up to Praça do Rossio.

The colourful **Alfama** district is reached by heading to the right along the north side of Praça do Comércio, turning up Rua da Madalena and then taking any of the roads uphill to the right. These lead to the cathedral, **Sé** (open Sun–Mon 9am–5pm, Tues–Sat 9am–7pm; admission fee to cloister), and into

Trams up to the Bairro Alto

central Alfama, with its narrow streets, medieval and Moorish-influenced buildings, wrought-iron balconies with flowers trailing or washing flapping on lines, and its mix of small shops and bars.

Across the northern corner of Alfama is the **Castelo de São Jorge** (St George's Castle; open daily Apr–Sept 9am–9pm, Oct–Mar 9am–6pm; free), the city's original Moorish fortress – which has with fine views across the city and the Tagus.

Situated on the other, western, side of Baixa is **Bairro Alto**, another historic district with narrow streets, which is now a wealthy residential district. It can be reached on foot or by tram. The **Elevador de Santa Justa**, an 100-year-old lift, near **Praça do Rossio** (Rossio Square) no longer gives access, as it once did, to the Bairro Alto, but you can ride up and down in the ornate carriage of this wonderful iron structure, just for fun and enjoy the views from the top. There's a café at the top, too.

Other Districts of Lisbon

Other major sights you may want to visit include the **Fundação Gulbenkian** (open Wed–Sun 10am–6pm; admission fee except on Sun), showcasing the impressive fine and decorative arts collection of Armenian oil billionaire Calouste Gulbenkian; and, in western district known as Belém (Bethlehem), the Manueline **Mosteiro dos Jerónimos** (open May–Sept Tues–Sun 10am–6pm, Oct–Apr Tues–Sun 10am–5pm; admission fee for cloisters), the **Padrão dos Descobri-**

mentos (Monument of the Discoveries) and the elaborate riverside **Torre de Belém** (Belém Tower); this 16th-century tower once stood in the Tagus to defend the city's ships but was left high and dry when the course of the river changed after the 1755 earthquake.

If you have time, other sights in Lisbon include the stunning architecture and the Oceanarium at the **Parque das Nações**, created for Lisbon's **Expo '98** and situated at the eastern end of the waterfront.

Royal Retreats outside Lisbon

Lisbon's countryside is rich in aristocratic palaces, built on the lush south-facing headlands of Portugal's Costa de Estorial. The **Palácio Nacional de Queluz** was built in the 18th-century as a summer retreat, in a fanciful baroque style, with echoes of Louis XIV's palace at Versailles. Costumed actors

Bélem's Monument of the Discoveries

roam the lovely romantic gardens so that you feel as if you have suddenly stepped back 250 years.

Royal families from all over Europe sought refuge at **Estoril** in World War II, earning it the name 'Coast of Kings'. Grand hotels and villas speak of that long-gone era, and now the fine sandy beach and glitzy casino attract all comers. The beach resort of **Cascais**, slightly further west, was also a favourite summer resort of the royal family during the early 20th century.

It's worth visiting the World Heritage site of **Sintra**, about half an hour from Lisbon, complete with a royal palace and Moorish Castle. The architectural highlight in Sintra itself is the **Palácio Nacional**, a former royal palace packed with treasures from the 14th century, when the Portuguese kings used it as a summer home. Even older is the **Castelo dos Mouros** (Moorish Castle) dating from the 8th-century Moorish conquest of Portugal, won back by Christians in 1147. There are great views from here and even better ones from the extraordinarily lavish **Palácio da Pena**, further up the hill.

Porto

Set at the mouth of the Douro River in the heart of wine-growing country, Portugal's second city, **Porto** (also known as Oporto, meaning 'the port'), has been a thriving port and commercial centre for over 3,000 years, and there is an air of elegance about its imposing squares, broad avenues and fine 18th-century merchants' mansions. The three bridges that span the deep river gorge are famous landmarks, the most notable being the two-tier Donna Maria Pia road bridge, by Gustave Eiffel.

> If time allows, visit one of the wine lodges in Porto's Ribeira district. You'll be given a brief history of port wine – discovered when merchants added brandy to Douro red wine to preserve the wine for shipment – and invited to taste the products.

The characterful quayside district of Porto's Cais da Ribeira

As you arrive in port, look out for *barcos rabelos*, traditional flat-bottomed boats that once brought port wine down from the Douro Valley to Ribeira's wine lodges.

The main port is on the south side of the Douro. Further along the seafront is Leixoes, Porto's seaside resort, which has an artificial harbour created in the 19th century to relieve congestion from the crowded quays along the Douro. The Dom Luis I bridge is the most direct link from the port to Ribeira, the oldest district and home to Porto's famous port cellars.

Medieval **Ribeira**, on the river's north bank, is more scenic than the modern city of Porto; it's well worth exploring, particularly around the 12th-century **Sé** (Cathedral) in Terreiro del Sé. More riches are to be found at the **Palácio do Bisbo**, the former Archbishop's Palace in the cathedral square. Now a museum, it contains fine silver and pewter work and a collection of European and Oriental ceramics. Head north along Avenida Dom A. Henriques, then left along Rua dos Clérigos and you'll spot the soaring tower of the magnificent 18th-century **Igreja dos Clérigos**. To the west of the tower, near Rua de Restauraçao, is the **Nacional Museu Soares dos Reis** (open Wed–Sun and Tues am; admission fee). Once the residence of Portugal's royal family, it now houses 16th-century paintings and works by the 19th-century sculptor Antonio Soares dos Reis.

Portimão

⚓ **Portimão** is a medieval city in Portugal's Algarve. While most visitors come for golf, sand and sun, the town is still a commercial port and the region's most important sardine canning centre. It's also known for deep-sea sport fishing and, along the estuary, bird-watching.

Ships have to sail into the river mouth to dock. You'll see the massive sandstone cliffs and wind-sculpted rock formations of the Algarve beaches as you approach, as well as the modern development strung out along the shoreline. Look out for the sand-coloured ruins of 16th-century Fortaleza de Santa Catarina on Praia da Rocha. Only small ships can dock in the port – others use tenders to ferry passengers ashore. Most cruise lines run shuttles to the town centre and to the beach, 3.5km (5 miles) from the centre. Most of Portimão's local colour is down by the port, a great place to try the local speciality of *sardinhas grelhadas* (smoky, grilled sardines) at any one of the dockside restaurants.

In the centre of town, Largo 1° de Dezembro is a 19th-century park with ten benches decorated with splendid blue-and-white *azulejos* (ceramic tiles), each illustrating a pivotal event in the history of Portugal. Along Rua Machado dos Santos is the handsome, yellow-and-white **Igreja de Nossa Senhora da Conceição**, sitting atop a small hill and incline of steps. Constructed in the 15th century, this church has a beautiful Gothic portico with carved capitals.

Madeira

Known as the Garden Island because of the richly varied plant life that thrives in its sub-tropical climate, **Madeira** has long been a popular destination – for British holiday-makers in particular. Never too hot in the summer, nor too cold in the winter, it retains a genteel appeal. Occasional attempts to attract younger visitors have failed because what makes the island so special has nothing to do with nightlife or beach parties and everything to do with scenery, shopping and sightseeing. Inland, there are some spectacular views from high points; along the coast there may be no beaches but there is a series of picturesque fishing villages that have inspired artists to travel many kilometres to paint them.

Madeira is either visited on an Atlantic Islands itinerary (Canaries plus Madeira), en route from the UK to the Mediterranean or, occasionally, on a transatlantic itinerary to

Madeira's pretty Câmara de Lobos is still an active fishing village

and from the Caribbean, but the stay is always for a full day. Usually, ships leave in the early evening. Occasionally, a ship will dock at the neighbouring island of Porto Santo, which has the beaches Madeira lacks, but little else.

Funchal

⚓ The approach to the harbour at the capital, **Funchal**, which lies at the heart of a half moon-shaped bay, is pretty rather than spectacular. As the dock area is right by the city centre, there is an excellent view of the town and the wooded hills above. From the dock, turn right and it is only around a 10- to 15-minute walk either past a yacht marina lined with seafood restaurants on Avenida do Mar or past the tourist information centre on the parallel Avenida Arriaga, into the centre of Funchal. Along the coast to the left are most of the main hotels including Reid's, which has become a visitor attraction in its own right. Buses or reasonably priced taxis run along the coast road.

Historic Funchal viewed from Pico dos Barcelos

About half the island's quarter-million population lives in Funchal, making it one of Portugal's largest cities, but it has more the feel of a country town. It is certainly walkable, with most of the more interesting buildings and shops in and around the main square, the **Praça do Município** – where there is a 17th-century church and an 18th-century palace (now the Town Hall – Câmara Municipal). Nearby is the art museum at **Quinta das Cruzes** (open Tues–Sat 10am–12.30pm, 2.30–5.30pm, Sun 10am–12.30pm; free), with attractive gardens that are open to the public.

Further inland, the narrow cobblestone streets become much steeper and are only for determined walkers. A short taxi ride, however, will take you to the magnificent **Jardím Botânico** on Camiho do Meiro.

The picturesque, traditional fishing village of **Câmara de Lobos**, 5km (3 miles) from Funchal, has a wonderful bay and offers some panoramic views from the nearby Pico da Torre.

Basket weaving and willow work are major export trades in Madeira, and you'll find an outstanding array of wicker items for sale on the island. Several factories allow tourist shoppers to see wicker-work in the making, an activity more interesting than it sounds: items are crafted not only with the hands and feet, but, at times, with the teeth too.

Helicopters are used for some sightseeing tours organised by the cruise lines. A visit to the highest point on the island – and Europe's tallest sea cliff – **Cabo Girao**, may be combined with a trip to the Botanical Gardens, followed by a toboggan ride from **Monte** into Funchal.

Spain

Climate Mainland Spain's Mediterranean coast has hot summers and mild winters. Winter rains are often interspersed with brilliant sunshine. Strong winds can be persistent along the Costa Brava. The Canary Islands are warm year round.

Time Zone One hour ahead of GMT except for the Canary Islands, which are +1 in winter, +2 in summer.

Opening Times Most shops open 9.30/10am–1.30/2pm and 4.30/5–8pm. Large stores apart, many shops close on Saturday afternoon during the summer.

What to Buy Good-quality craftwork, including hand-sewn, embroidered Manila shawls, leather and suede goods and earthenware pottery. Cultured pearls, intricate fans, baskets, silver jewellery, ceramics and rugs.

Money Matters Euro

Public Holidays 1, 6 January, 19 March, Good Friday, 1 May, 5 August, 12 October, 1 November, 6, 8 and 25 December. Also local holidays in honour of patron saints.

Etiquette Wearing miniskirts or shorts may restrict admission to churches and other religious sites. Shoulders should be covered; some churches provide shawls.

Tipping Service is rarely added to a restaurant bill; 10 percent is appropriate. A 10 percent tip is usual for taxis.

Hazards and Security Sunscreen and hat are vital in summer. Though food hygiene has improved enormously, beware of eating fish on Sunday or Monday, as it may not be fresh. Be on your guard against purse-snatchers and pickpockets in markets and other crowded places.

Drugs and Medicines It is advisable to bring any prescription medicines you need. Foreign prescriptions are not honoured.

Emergency Telephone Numbers To contact the national police telephone 091; municipal police 092; emergency medical care 061.

The bullring in Ronda

SPAIN

The glittering coast of Spain is visited by almost all cruise lines operating in the western Mediterranean. On mainland Spain, visitors will be struck by the different cultural influences: Barcelona looks to northern Europe, while more southerly ports, such as Málaga, betray Spain's strong, early links with North Africa. Some ports are primarily used as transit points for accessing inland sites of particular interest; others are destinations in themselves. The Balearic Islands, which are also on many cruise liners' itineraries, have an atmosphere all their own, from Catalan-influenced Palma de Mallorca, to Maó, Menorca's capital, which has not shaken off all remnants of its past under British rule. Head south from Portugal's island of Madeira and you come to Spain's Atlantic islands, the Canaries, closer to the Moroccan coast. Above them, between Africa and Europe, the Straits of Gibraltar herald the Mediterranean.

Málaga's Plaza de la Constitución

Málaga

Málaga is the principal city 🏴 on the Costa del Sol. It has the main airport and is a busy port and a thriving commercial centre, quite different in character from the mass of holiday resorts either side of its boundaries. Most cruise lines visiting the western Mediterranean call at Málaga; some berth overnight here, giving passengers a chance to fit in more than one excursion. It's a 15- to 20-minute walk from the quayside to the city centre around Plaza de la Constitución and Calle Puerta de Mar, where there are plenty of bars, boutiques and department stores.

Málaga is overlooked by a ruined, hilltop fortress, the 9th-century Gibralfaro. Just below it is the 11th-century Alcazaba, another fine relic from the Moorish occupation.

The park by the port is grimy and somewhat depressing. Head for the lovely gardens around the **Alcazaba**, which also houses the local archaeological museum. Climb the steep path on the eastern side to the castle (or take a taxi) for views of the coast. Back in the centre, among streets of elegant, late 19th-century buildings, the **Cathedral**, on Calle Molina de Lários, dates from the 16th century and is built on the site of a mosque in a mix of Gothic, baroque and Renaissance styles. The **Museo Picasso** (open Mon–Sat 10am–8pm; admission fee) houses one of the world's finest collections of the artist's work.

Málaga is used by most cruise passengers as a base from which to tour Andalucía. If you wish to explore independently, it's easy to hire a car and take off into the hills. Alternatively, several tours are operated by the cruise lines.

Granada and the Alhambra

The most popular tour from Málaga is to the magnificent **Alhambra** at Granada. Alhambra means 'The Red', a reference to the red-brown bricks used by the Moorish rulers of Andalucía to build this stunning complex, which rises precipitously from the deep gorge of the Darro River.

Within the walls of the Alhambra, there are four main areas to explore: the Alcazaba (Fortress), the Casa Real Vieja (Old Royal Palace), the Casa Real Nueva (New Royal Palace) and the Generalife (Summer Gardens). The Old Royal Palace is the highlight of the monument, with its complex of courtyards, patios, fountains, pools and sumptuously tiled halls. It is perfectly complemented by the Generalife, whose terraced gardens form a series of outdoor rooms, delineated by neatly clipped cypress hedges, full of luxuriant blooms and gentle fountains.

The Alhambra, one of the highlights of a trip to southern Spain

Granada itself is one of the most stunning cities in Spain. Backed by the snow-capped peaks of the Sierra Nevada, it was the capital of Moorish Spain from 1232 until 1492, when the Catholic Monarchs completed their ruthless campaign to drive the Moors back to their African homeland.

> During the Spanish Civil War, nationalist sympathisers in Ronda were hurled to their deaths in the Tajo Gorge below, an event recalled by Ernest Hemingway in his novel *For Whom the Bell Tolls*.

Ronda

Other popular excursions from Málaga include Ronda, Mijas and Marbella. **Ronda** is a spectacular town that clings dramatically to a clifftop, 150m (500ft) above the Tajo Gorge. Ronda's Puente Nueve (New Bridge) spans the gorge and connects the new centre with the old town, from where Ronda's Moorish kings and its Christian conquerors ruled at the Palacio de Mondragón. The town's neoclassical Plaza de Toros (bullring) is one of the oldest in Spain and is venerated as the cradle of the *corrida* (bullfight).

Mijas and Marbella

Andalucía is famed for its enchanting *pueblos blancos*, beautiful whitewashed hill towns where the way of life seems to have changed little since Moorish times. **Mijas** is a perfect example of one of these, complete with cobbled streets and balconies decorated with hanging baskets. Parts of the village are touristy, with souvenir shops selling the usual fare; the rustic upper part of the town is likely to be less crowded than the centre. To get up there, you may wish to take the local form of transport, a *burro taxi* (donkey taxi), as traffic is banned from the centre. Mijas has Spain's only square bullring, and, opposite, beautifully tended gardens slope down to a clifftop *mirador* (viewpoint), from where there are fine views all along the coast.

From Mijas, it is a short step to the glamorous resort of **Marbella**, famed for its long stretch of beach. The city's beautiful Casa Antiguo (Old Town) has been carefully preserved as a pedestrian district of tiny squares and whitewashed houses hung with colourful bourgainvillea.

Cuevas de Nerja

The **Cuevas de Nerja** (Nerja Caves) are the second most-visited sight in Andalucía after the Alhambra. The cave complex lies east of Málaga and was discovered in 1959 by local boys who stumbled upon them while hunting. Archaeologists have found human remains dating back 30,000 years, making this one of Europe's oldest inhabited sites. Beautifully lit, the caves create a fairytale world of stalactites and stalagmites. The astonishing main cave, 800m (2,624ft) in length, has been dubbed the Cathedral of the Costa del Sol. It contains the world's largest stalactite, a whopping 32m (105ft) long, with a diameter of 18m (59ft). Allow half a day for a visit here.

Cádiz

The ancient city of **Cádiz**, isolated at the end of a very narrow peninsula of land running parallel to the coast, was founded by the Phoenicians in 1100BC and is considered to be Spain's oldest town. In fact, the amazing amalgam of history is not readily apparent, with only the remains of the Roman theatre giving much evidence of its age.

Sights in the city include the excellent **Museo de Cádiz**, which exhibits Phoenician and Roman artefacts and paintings by Francisco Zurbarán, as well as local crafts. Overlooking the ocean, the **cathedral** gives evidence of an extended construction period between 1772 and 1838, and has a landmark dome that glitters like gold in the sunshine. (The artist Murillo fell fatally from a scaffold when painting an altarpiece in 1816.) The curious and unusual **Oratorio de la Santa Cueva** has underground chapels dating from 1783. Of more interest is the domed upper chapel added in 1796. Five spectacular paintings adorn its ceiling – three are fine examples of Goya's work.

Jerez de la Frontera

The largest town in the province of Cádiz, Jerez owes its fame to sherry and horses. The English corrupted Jerez to 'sherry' and exported the locally produced wine. Several of the many *bodegas* (wineries) in Jerez welcome tourists to their dark, aromatic halls, and offer free tastings. As for the horses, the **Real Escuela Andaluza del Arte Ecuestre** (Royal Andalucían School of Equestrian Art) puts its star pupils through a splendid choreographed dressage show at noon every Thursday and on Tuesdays between March and October, plus Fridays in August (Thursdays only in winter) and there are weekday training sessions. The highlight of the equestrian calendar is the May Spring Horse Fair, when the town is full of dandified horses and their finely dressed riders. An 11th-century mosque is found inside the **Alcázar** (fortress), and the nearby 18th-century Colegiata holds a precious image of Christ of the Vineyards.

> In Andalucía the palest and driest styles of sherry – *manzanilla* and *fino* – are drunk chilled as an appetiser or an accompaniment to *tapas*.

Seville

When Julius Caesar arrived in Spain in 45BC, **Seville** (Sevilla) was a thriving riverside settlement, but under the Romans it became a major town. Two Roman emperors – Hadrian and Trajan – were born in nearby Itálica. Subsequently capital of the Visigoths and then of a Moorish *taifa*, Sevilla finally fell to Fernando III in 1248. A monopoly of trade with the New World brought the city to its peak during the Golden Age. 'Madrid is the capital of Spain,' the saying went, 'but Sevilla is the capital of the world.' Without doubt, Sevilla, the capital of Andalucía and Spain's fourth-largest city, is the most important city in the region. Its name is evocative of bull-fighting, flamenco, the operatic temptress Carmen and many icons that represent Spain in visitors' minds.

The city's two most prominent monuments are located around the Plaza del Triunfo. The **cathedral** (open Mon–Sat

Seville's 15th-century cathedral, built on the site of a mosque

9.30am–4.30pm, Sun 2.30–7pm; admission fee includes entry to the Giralda, free on Sun) is the largest Gothic church in the world, and among cathedrals is only surpassed in size by St Peter's in Rome and St Paul's in London. It was begun in 1401, after the great mosque was razed, and completed in just over a century. The new building followed the ground plan of the old mosque, accounting for its unusual broad, rectangular form. Massive without, and richly decorated within, the cathedral contains more than 30 chapels, including the central **Capilla Mayor** with its Flemish Plateresque altarpiece, and the **Capilla Real** (Royal Chapel), last resting place of Fernando III, the 'King-Saint' who delivered Seville from the hands of the infidel. The stunning altar screen is overlaid with 3,500kg (7,700lb) of gold. Christopher Columbus (Cristobal Colón) is interred in the ornate 19th-century sarcophagus by the south entrance. His remains were transferred to Sevilla from Havana in 1898, when Cuba won its independence from Spain.

On the north side of the cathedral is the **Patio de los Naranjos** (Court of the Orange Trees), the ceremonial court-yard of the old mosque with its original ablutions fountains. The bell tower of the cathedral, the **Giralda** tower – Seville's

---

Flamenco

Flamenco is an ancient art form, combining elements of Visigothic, Moorish and Gypsy music. There are two distinct types; the *cante jondo* (deep song), an intense outpouring of emotion; and the animated *cante chico* (light song). There are also different varieties of flamenco dance (including the *tango*, *fandango*, *farruca* and *zambra*), performed to the staccato rhythms and counter-rhythms of the castanets, hand clapping (*palmadas*) and finger snapping (*pitos*), as well as furious heel-drumming (*zapateado*). There is no need to speak Spanish to enjoy the spectacle – you simply have to feel the music.

most famous landmark – dates from 1184, and was the original mosque's minaret. The exterior is finely decorated with typical *sebka* design work, while the interior has a series of 35 gently rising ramps (designed for horses to climb – Fernando III rode his horse to the top following the Reconquest in 1248) leading to an observation platform 70m (230ft) in the air and offering a tremendous panorama across the city.

The **Real Alcázar** is a major monument of mid-14th century Mudéjar architecture, combining Moorish, Gothic and Renaissance elements (open Apr–Sept 9.30am–8pm, Sun 9.30am–6pm; Oct–Mar 9.30am–6pm, Sun 9.30am–2.30pm; admission fee). Built by Moorish craftsmen under Christian rule, in the reign of Pedro the Cruel, the palace and its courtyards incorporate fragments of a Moorish fortress, and blend Christian motifs with Moorish designs. Not to be missed are the gardens, an oasis of calm.

The Puerta de León, the main entrance to the Real Alcázar

Nearby, on the banks of the river, is another of Sevilla's icons. The Moorish **Torre del Oro** (Tower of Gold) is named after the gold-coloured tiles that once covered the walls of this early 13th-century tower – all that remains of Seville's medieval fortifications.

Other attractions include the labyrinthine streets of the **Barrio de Santa Cruz**, which border the Alcázar. On the edge of this district, Mudéjar delights await in the 16th-century **Casa de Pilatos** (open daily 9am–8pm, closes 6pm Oct–June; admission fee, free Tues 1–5pm). Art lovers may wish to visit the **Museo de Bellas Artes** (open Tues 3–8pm, Wed–Sat 9am–8pm, Sun 9am–2pm; admission fee) with its fine art collection.

Barcelona

⚓ **Barcelona** is the capital of Catalunya, an autonomous self-governing region of northeastern Spain with its own language (Catalan), traditions and history. It is also Spain's second city, a stylish metropolis by the sea, on the stretch of the Mediterranean known as the Costa Brava (Wild Coast) because of its many unspoiled coves.

Flower sellers on the Rambla

La Rambla

Barcelona is a city that dares to be different, not only in fostering the eccentric talents of such Catalan artists as Picasso, Dalí and Miró, but also in pursuing a hedonistic, flamboyant lifestyle, as is clear to anyone who wanders up the city's famous main promenade, **La Rambla** (often referred to as Las Ramblas as it's made up of five sections). Rambla itself comes from the Arabic for gully – it was once a dried-up river bed. The tree-shaded street is out of bounds to traffic and, being 1km (⅔ mile) long, is perfect for a stroll.

The Rambla starts at the port end of town, by the **Mirador a Colóm** (Columbus Monument). The first stretch, the Rambla de Santa Mónica, has a craft market; the next stretch is a popular haunt of street mime artists.

Plas de l'Os, with its mosaic pavement designed by Miró, marks the mid-point of the Rambla, and up on the

Fresh produce at the Boquería

left, set back from the street is **La Boquería**, officially known as Mercat Sant Josep. It's a feast for the senses, with fruit, vegetables, meat, fish, olive oil, clothing and leather goods for sale.

Picturesque Flower Alley, the Rambla de los Flors, is the place to buy books and roses – the combination is deliberate, for it is tradition that men buy ladies a rose, and ladies buy men a book on 23 April, the feast of the city's patron saint, Sant Jordi (St George). Stallholders along the Rambla dels Estudis – unofficially known as the Rambla dels Ocells, the Rambla of Birds – sell all sorts of domestic pets, including caged song birds. The last stretch of all, the Rambla de Canaletes, is where football fans, fanatical in their devotion to their home team, FC Barcelona, meet before and after the big match. Drink from the fountain of Canaletes and you are sure to return to this city some time in your life.

The Rambla ends at **Plaça de Catalunya**, the symbolic centre of the city because it was so often the scene of huge demonstrations in favour of Catalan autonomy in the 1970s. Having won their right to regional autonomy, the people of Barcelona now come here to enjoy themselves by strolling arm in arm among the monumental fountains, or to shop in El Corte Inglés, Spain's best-known department store.

Antoni Gaudí

Barcelona is renowned for the work of architect Antoni Gaudí, whose buildings are typified by naturalistic lines and motifs and a rebellion against rigid forms. Much of Gaudí's work was financed by textile manufacturer Count Eusebi Güell. The **Palau Güell** (Carrer Nou de la Rambla; closed for renovation until 2007) previews many aspects of Gaudí's work. Güell also gave his name to **Parc Güell** (open daily, Nov–Feb 10am–6pm, Mar and Oct till 7pm, Apr and Sept till 8pm, May and Aug till 9pm), which features sinuous steps and decorative mosaics.

An exhibition in the loft of another of Gaudí's designs, an apartment block known as **La Pedrera** (Passeig de Gràcia; open daily 10am–8pm; admission fee), illustrates the architect's working methods and offers fabulous views over the city. Built in 1904–6 the sinuous **Casa Batlló** (Passeig de Gracia; Mon–Sat 9am–2pm, Sun 9am–8pm; admission fee) is remarkable for its façade covered with scraps of broken plate and tile, a decorative technique called *trencadis*. However, Gaudí's masterpiece is the **Sagrada Família** (open daily Nov–Feb 9am–6pm, Mar and Sept–Oct till 7pm, April and Aug till 8pm); the cathedral is still a work in progress (due for completion in 2026; admission fee).

Gaudí died in 1926, aged 74, and is buried in the crypt of the Sagrada Família. He was a pious, conservative man, despite his innovations, and during his last years he lived in a room on the site, obsessed with the project. When passers-by discovered the architect run over by a tram in the nearby street and took him to hospital, the doctors, unable at first to identify him, thought the dishevelled old man was a tramp. When it was discovered who he was, the entire city turned out for his funeral.

Central Districts

Barcelona's other districts fan out from this central square. To the north, in the district known as **L'Eixample**, is another of the city's symbols – Antonio Gaudí's extraordinary **Sagrada Familia** (Cathedral of the Holy Family, *see box opposite*). The Casa Batlló and La Perdrera are also in this district.

As well as the Sagrada Família, Barcelona has another fine cathedral, in the oldest part of the city, the **Barri Gótic** (Gothic Quarter), which lies to the east of the Rambla. This is another great place for a stroll through quiet, narrow, traffic-free alleys.

Work in progress: Gaudí's extraordinary Sagrada Família

The cathedral, **La Seu** (Plaça de la Seu; open daily 8.30am–1.30pm, 4–7.30pm; free), a masterpiece of Gothic artistry, has a lovely cloister, shaded by palms and scented orange trees and home to a noisy flock of white geese. These commemorate another of the city's patron saints, the little girl martyr, St Eulália. She was tortured and put to death by the Roman rulers of Barcelona, and the 13 white geese symbolise her purity and the age at which she died.

Some of the most beautiful Gothic architecture and most fascinating medieval corners of Barcelona lie just outside the Barri Gòtic. In this area, in Carrer Moncada, is one of the city's best museums, the **Museu Picasso** (Carrer Moncada; open Tues–Sat 10am–8pm, Sun 10am–3pm; admission fee). Picasso had a great attachment to Barcelona, where he grew up, and while he did not want his work exhibited here during Franco's

Designed by Lluís Domènech i Montaner, Barcelona's Palau de la Música (Sant Francesc de Paula 2) is the perfect expression of the architectural style known as *modernisme*. A UNESCO World Heritage site, the concert hall is an explosion of mosaics, tiles, stained glass, enamel, sculpture and carving.

regime, he relented towards the end of that period and, in 1970, donated over 2,000 of his works. The museum is housed in a series of adjoining medieval palaces.

Monjuïc

Montjuïc, the hill to the west of the city, came into its own as the site of Barcelona's 1929 International Exhibition, and was the site for the core events of the 1992 Olympic Games. For many years its 210m (689ft) summit, with panoramic views of the city and harbour, and outstanding complex of museums and sports facilities have made the hill a favourite spot.

A number of hangar-type halls, the premises of the Barcelona Trade Fairs organisation, line a central avenue leading upwards to the vast **Palau Nacional**, the fair's Spanish pavilion. To the right is the **Pavelló Mies van der Rohe** (open Mon–Fri 10am–8pm, Sat–Sun 11am–7pm), built for the 1929 Exposition.

Montjuïc is home to the **Fundació Joan Miró** (open Jun–Sept Tues–Sat 10am–8pm, Thurs till 9.30pm, Sun 10am–2.30pm; Nov–May Tues–Sat 10am–7pm, Thurs till 9.30pm, Sun 10am–2.30pm; admission fee), home to 10,000 works by this Catalan artist. The building was purpose-designed by architect Josep Luís Sert, a close friend of Miró.

Montserrat

Excursions from Barcelona include the dramatically set monastery at **Montserrat**, 40km (25 miles) northwest; it can also be reached independently, by train and cable car. The monastery sits on the ridge of an unusual rock formation 1,135m (3,725ft) above the Llobregat River valley. It is the spiritual home of Catalunya and one of Spain's main pilgrimage sites due to its Black Madonna (*La Moreneta*), a statue said to have been made by St Luke and brought to Barcelona by St Peter. In 1808, Napoleon's troops destroyed the original 12th-century monastery; the present one dates from 1874. Montserrat is still an active Benedictine place of worship; visitors may only enter the basilica, Gothic cloister and museum. If possible, time your visit to concide with a recital by the Escalonia Boys' Choir (Mon–Sat at 1pm and 6.45pm; Sun and high feast days noon; no recitals in July).

The monastery at Montserrat, a name that means 'serrated mountain'

Palma's cathedral dominates the harbour

THE BALEARIC ISLANDS

The Balearics, off the northeast coast of Spain, form a Spanish autonomous province. Historically part of Catalunya, they have their own versions of the Catalan language, and the people are fiercely proud of their island identity. Although sometimes linked with the tackier kind of package holidays, the Balearics are beautiful, with many peaceful corners and historic towns and, in Mallorca, rugged mountain scenery.

Mallorca

Mallorca's history dates to the Bronze Age. Over the millennia, visitors, invaders and conquerors have all left marks on the island; there are architectural remains from the Phoenicians, Carthaginians, Arabs, Greeks and Romans, who all suffered attacks by the Vandals from the north. Since then, the 13th-century Catalan conquerors and, more recently, tourists have brought their own contributions to the island's culture.

Palma

The city of **Palma** is sprawling and busy, but most of the highlights are concentrated in a relatively small area, in and around the old town. Most cruise ships visit Palma for a full day, and many stay as late as midnight.

A strip of land appears on the horizon about three hours before the ship actually reaches Palma. It grows larger and closer until the grey craggy cliffs tumble into the sea and the golden sands come into view, splashed with white spray.

As the ship slows to turn into the harbour, the bulk of the **Castell de Bellver** commands the bay from the nearest hill to the west, and the Gothic slabs of the cathedral buttresses stand out from the east of town, dominating the bay from all sides. At the terminal, passengers disembark at the upper level, and either take coaches from the ground floor for excursions, or take the covered walkway for about 10 minutes to the bus terminus, where taxis also await. Boats can be rented from here, too.

It is an easy walk from the bus terminus to **Porto Pi Centro**, a retail-drome housing some famous stores, including Zara, Mango and Disney. **Avinguda Jaume III**, in the city centre, is the major shopping street, lined with chic leather and clothing shops as well as department stores, including a big branch of Spain's biggest, El Corte

Mallorcans speak both Spanish (Castilian) and Mallorquí, a variant of Catalan, which is now the official language. Most signs and street names are written in Mallorquí, and this is the language people choose to speak among themselves (it's also used in schools). However, they are a communicative people, quite happy to address outsiders in Spanish, and the high number of seasonal workers who come here from the mainland ensures that Spanish is spoken everywhere.

Inglés. Also on this street is an outlet of the quirky shoe company, **Camper**, which is based in Inca, in the centre of the island; and **Perlas Majorica**, manufacturers of Mallorcan cultured (artificial) pearls.

A taxi ride into the centre takes about 10 minutes. Taxis are fairly expensive, but plentiful. Along the quayside as you travel in, the well-preserved city walls stand proud, topped by the occasional windmill. The road is lined with bars designed to appeal to boating and cruising visitors.

At the far side of the bay is **La Seu** (cathedral; open Mon–Fri 10am–5.30pm, Sat 10am–2.30pm; admission fee for museum and treasury).

Sunlight streams through the cathedral's rose window

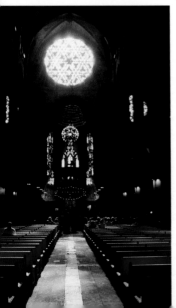

Begun in 1230 but not completed until four centuries later, it has flying buttresses in Catalan-Gothic style and a much later wrought-iron altar canopy *(baldachino)*, by Gaudí. The lovely **Palau de l'Almudaina** (open Mon–Fri 10am–6.30pm and Sat am; admission fee) is to the west of the cathedral. In the **Parc de la Mar** below, the cathedral is mirrored in a lake, and in the nearby **S'Hort del Rei**, a lovely Arabic-style garden, there are fountains, pools, flowers, shrubs and trees.

From behind the cathedral, sightseeing tours are offered in carriages drawn by tired-looking horses. On the corner of Carrer Palau Reial the handsome **Palau March Museu** (open Mon–Fri Nov–Mar 10am–6pm, Apr–Oct 10am–6.30pm, Sat all year 10am–2pm; admission fee) exhibits excellent modern sculpture on its palm-lined terrace, and paintings in the interior. An elegant café serves particularly good coffee. Along arcaded Carrer Palau Reial, past some smart cafés, you reach the impressive Ajuntament (town hall) in the Plaça del Cort, in the centre of which stands an ancient, gnarled olive tree. Off to the right, in a large, airy, square with outdoor cafés and bars, is the fine 14th-century church of **Santa Eulàlia**. To the other side of the **Plaça de Cort**, elegant art nouveau buildings house designer, antique and technology shops.

Lush Vegetation

The flora of Mallorca is as diverse as the landscape. There are cultivated olives, almonds, apricot and citrus trees; holm oaks and pines flourish in mountainous regions, with rosemary, lavender and heather turning the hillsides purple. There are sturdy palm trees growing at sea level, and bougainvillaea brightening up village walls.

On the far side of the cathedral, cobbled streets too narrow for cars form the **medieval quarter**. It's best visited outside the hot hours of siesta, as it can be quite airless. These attractive alleyways are fascinating; large doorways in heavy, ochre-coloured walls give tantalising glimpses into shady courtyards, usually with ferns and palm trees, and stone staircases leading to upper levels. Apartments, galleries and a few small museums are housed inside these intriguing entrances. Museums include the **Museu de Mallorca** (Carrer Portella; open Tues–Sat Apr–Sept 10am–2pm, 5–8pm, Oct–Mar 10am–1pm, 4–6pm, Sun all year 10am–2pm; admission fee), an excellent history museum; and the **Casa Museu J. Torrens Lladó** (open mid-Sept–mid-Jun Tues–Fri 10am–6pm, mid-Jun–mid-Sept Tues–Fri 11am–7pm; Sat 10am–2pm; admission fee), home and studio of the 20th-century Catalan painter.

The 10th-century **Banys Arabs** (Arab baths) close by are a delight. The serene courtyard with a well, towering palms, flowers and ferns, along with a few tables and chairs and a soft-drinks machine, are perfect for a picnic. To the side of the courtyard, the baths themselves are entered through a keyhole-shaped Arabic arch. The brick beehive dome of the baths is supported by a ring of columns. This is the only complete Moorish building remaining on the island.

Valldemossa

Tours from Palma may include the beautiful hilltop town of **Valldemossa**, where the composer Chopin and the writer Georges Sand lived, the 18th-century manor house at Son Marroig, and a full-day visit to the east coast Caves of Drach. Chopin and Sands didn't seem to be particularly happy at Valldemossa: Chopin was unwell, the weather was miserable, and the villagers disapproved of Sands' eccentric habit of wearing men's clothing and smoking cigars.

Stunning Valldemossa

Cala en Turqueta, a typical Menorcan beach

Menorca

Menorca came late to the tourism industry, missing out on the unregulated excesses of the 1960s and 1970s. Since it has been discovered, planning controls and environmental awareness have largely prevented development of the more unacceptable kind. Menorca is only one-fifth the size of Mallorca, with a tenth of the population, and receives only about an eighth of its bigger sister's visitors. It is also the only Balearic Island to have been designated a UNESCO biosphere reserve, defined as 'a place of important natural and cultural heritage, where economic development is compatible with nature conservation' – a title of which it is very proud.

The capital and largest town, Maó, and the former capital, Ciutadella, are on opposite coasts. Resort development is restricted to a handful of coves and beaches on the southeast and west coasts. One main road, 44km (26 miles) long, links the two cities.

Maó's Sant Francesc d'Assís

Maó

Maó (Mahon), has one of the best harbours in the Mediterranean – hence it was seized by the British in 1708 in the War of the Spanish Succession. They moved the capital from Ciutadella to Maó, and kept the island intermittently for nearly a century. In 1802 Menorca reverted to Spanish rule.

Ships usually spend a whole day here. Be up on deck for the approach to Maó, as the white houses clinging to its rocky coast make a dazzling sight, and the old town rising above the harbour is impressive. The docks are close to the old town, which is reached via steps and a curving road (Ses Voltes) leading up from the sea.

Maó's main sights are easily seen on foot in an hour or so. At the top of Ses Voltes, in the busy **Plaça d'Espanya**, looms the Església del Carmen. A lively food, clothes and souvenir market is held daily in the adjoining cloister, the **Claustre del Carme**, where there is also a café with a sunny terrace offering lovely views over the harbour. To the other side of Ses Voltes, in the **Plaça de Sa Constitució** is the **Església de Santa Maria**, which dates from the 13th century but was completely rebuilt in the 18th. It's worth a visit for the Catalan-Gothic interior, and its organ, one of the world's largest. Another imposing building in the square, the **Ajuntament** (town hall), was built on the site of a medieval fortress, of which little survives.

Parròquia de Sant Francesc d'Assís (open daily; free) is a short walk away. Completed in 1792, it was the church of a Franciscan monastery, of which only the cloister remains; this houses the extensive collections of the **Museu de Menorca**

(open summer Tues–Sat 10am–2pm, 5–8pm, Sun 10am–2pm; admission fee). Exhibits range from *talayotic* (Balearic Bronze Age) finds to Greek and Roman amphorae, Islamic tiles and Spanish and British ceramics. Close by, the 15th-century **Port de Sant Roc** is Maó's only surviving medieval town gate.

It's enjoyable to stroll about admiring the fine Georgian houses, which are a legacy of British rule, and absorbing the atmosphere before settling down for lunch. The harbourside is lined with restaurants, many specialising in fish and seafood, others serving traditional dishes such as *caracoles con allioli* – snails in garlic mayonnaise – or *lechona* (roast suckling pig).

Binibeca-Vell and Ciutadella

Half-day tours from Maó normally include Binibeca Vell, a quaint, architect-designed village in the south, which has a range of shops, restaurants and bars.

The full-day Menorca tour takes in the island's old capital, **Ciutadella**, the Naveta des Tudons (the most famous of the prehistoric monuments that dot the island), the fishing village of Fornells (at the mouth of a spectacular bay) and Monte Toro, the island's highest point and its spiritual and geographical centre. From here, on a clear day, you can see Fornells and the distant outline of Mallorca.

Townhouses in Ciutadella, erstwhile capital of Menorca

THE CANARY ISLANDS

This archipelago of volcanic islands were called 'the Happy Islands' by the Romans because of their sunny, temperate climate. There are seven main islands in the group – Gran Canaria, Fuerteventura, Lanzarote, Tenerife, La Palma, La Gomera and El Hierro.

Try to eat ashore on the Canaries, as fish, fruits and vegetables are top quality, and recipes – a blend of Spanish, African and South American influences – are memorable. *Papas arrugadas*, potatoes boiled in their skins and served with *mojo rojo*, a sauce of oil, garlic, peppers and paprika, are delicious. Fresh Atlantic fish, grilled and served with *mojo verde* – a coriander and parsley version of the famous sauce – is also excellent, as is *flor de Guia*, the cheese made in Gran Canaria. For dessert, you can feast on locally grown bananas and on *morcillas dulces*, made with grapes, raisins and almonds. Recommended local wines are Malvasía from Lanzarote and the red wines of El Hierro, La Palma and Taraconte on Tenerife.

The Canaries are popular winter-sun destinations for UK cruise operators offering sailings from Dover or Southampton, and on these the islands are ports of call rather than home ports. However, Tenerife and Gran Canaria also feature as home ports for some repositioning cruises and fly-cruises.

Bird of paradise, the Canaries' adopted flower

Tenerife

The largest of the Canary Islands, **Tenerife** is scenically one of the most dramatic places in the world. Dominated by the vast Mt Teide, the island offers visitors varied scenery from beaches to pinewoods, lush banana plantations, spectacular verdant valleys and striking volcanic scenery in the Parque Nacional de las Cañadas del Teide, where you can take a cable car *(teleférico)* to the rim of the crater.

Santa Cruz

The capital and principal port, **Santa Cruz de Tenerife**, started life as a small fishing village but is now a sophisticated city with top-class bars and restaurants, interesting shops, fine architecture and good museums. Getting to it all on foot, though, can be a long haul,

Playa de las Teresitas and Tenerife's capital, Santa Cruz

depending on which part of the U-shaped harbour your ship has docked. It's easy from the bottom of the 'U' – just go through the port gates and you'll find the boulevard that runs to the city centre (and taxis right outside). But from one of the port's long quays, you'll face a 15-minute walk just to reach the port gates (though shuttle buses are sometimes laid on).

Outside the port gates you'll find the café-lined town-centre boulevard and, just off it, two or three streets selling bargain-priced electrical goods and CDs – Tenerife's speciality. Also on the waterfront is the **Plaza de España**, a good place to start exploring, as most of the city's sights and shops are in the streets leading inland from this square. Embroidery and lace-making are traditional island crafts, and island craft speciality shops include Artenerife by the port in Puerto de la Cruz and Artesanía El Sol in Santa Cruz. Cigars, hand-rolled from locally grown tobacco, local wines and Tenerife honey (*miel*) are interesting buys here.

As you face Plaza de España, the main bus station is to your left. Off to the right is the **Museo Municipal de Bellas Artes** (open Tues–Fri 10am–8pm, Sat–Sun 11am–4pm; free), which has some impressive paintings. Up Calle San Francisco is the **Museo Militar** (open Tues–Sun 10am–2pm; free), which houses El Tigre, the cannon whose shot shattered Nelson's arm in 1797. To the south of town is the 16th-century **Iglesia de Nuestra Señora de la Concepción** (church of the Immaculate Conception), the town's most important historical building. Nearby, the **Museo de la Naturaleza y el Hombre** (open Tues–Sun 9am–7pm; admission fee) has exhibits that

Teide, Spain's highest mountain *(see page 60)*

illustrate the lives and death rituals of the islands' earliest inhabitants; **Mercado de Nuestro Señora de Africa**, a colourful fruit, flower and vegetable market, is also well worth visiting.

On the main road near the port is the elegant **Auditorio**, home to the Tenerife Symphony Orchestra. Behind it, beyond the **Castillo San Juan**, is the **Parque Marítimo César Manrique** (open daily; admission fee), an area of seawater pools, with trees,

Toucan at Loro Parque

flowers and waterfalls. To the northeast of town is the long golden sweep of the **Playa de las Teresitas**, the city beach.

Other Attractions

Buses go directly from Santa Cruz bus station (check return times carefully) to the lovely seaside resort of **Puerto de la Cruz**, around 45 minutes' drive away. The main square is the **Plaza del Charco de los Camarones** at the heart of the historic district, surrounded by attractive buildings. To the east lies **Lago Martiánez** (open daily 9am–5pm; admission fee), an attractive seawater lido with fountains and palm-fringed sands, a pleasant alternative to the black-sand beaches.

A 5-minute taxi ride to the west of town is **Loro Parque** (open daily 9am–6pm; admission fee), a vast theme park with aquaria, dolphin pools, sea lions, an underwater tunnel and a bat cave. You can get a free train ride there from the Avenida de Venezuela (to the east of Plaza del Charco in Puerto de la Cruz); yellow tourist trains run every 20 minutes.

> **The national park that centres on towering Mt Teide is covered with the lunar landscapes of lava fields and full of extraordinary gnarled rock formations, most impressive of which are Los Roques de García.**

First-time visitors should not miss the **Parque Nacional de las Cañadas del Teide**, surrounding volcanic Teide, which, at 3,718m (12,198ft), is Spain's highest mountain. You can get close to the summit by the *teleférico* (cable car), 8km (5 miles) south of the park entrance and visitor centre. It's best to visit the park by a ship's tour, as it's hard to reach by bus and costly by taxi.

Other ship's tours include **Esperanza Forest** and the **Guimar pyramid** and **Risco Bello** aquatic garden.

Gran Canaria

Gran Canaria is the third-largest island in the Canaries, but its capital, Las Palmas, is the islands' biggest city, a buzzing place, with a huge port. In the south of the island is the resort of Playa del Inglés, with stunning beaches, and the dunes of Maspalomas. Inland, you'll fine old towns such as the banana capital of Arucas and historic Teror, while the island's volcanic interior is a landscape of mountains and gorges.

Las Palmas

⚓ **Las Palmas'** Santa Catalina terminal is a major hub for intra-island ferry services and cruise ships, so there is always plenty of activity as you arrive. City buses and those for other parts of the island leave from a bus station right in front of the terminal, where you'll also find lots of taxis.

Beside the port you'll see **El Muelle**, a shiny commercial centre that houses large stores and small boutiques. There are lots of shopping opportunities in the narrow streets on the other side of nearby **Parque Santa Catalina**, a palm-dotted square full of outdoor cafés. Here you can take advantage of Las Palmas' tax exemptions when buying watches, jewellery and electrical goods. Look carefully though – some things are no cheaper than you would get at home. For good-quality island crafts, go to the **Federación para el Desarrollo de la Artesanía Canaria** (FEDAC) in Calle Domingo J. Navarro, in the Triana district, where the pedestrianised shopping street of Calle Mayor de Triana has a wide variety of shops.

The best eating areas are along Playa de las Canteras and Vegueta *(see below)*. The former specialises in seafood, the latter has places serving typical island dishes. The Triana district also has some excellent, smart venues.

To get to the attractive district of **Triana,** take a bus from Plaza de Santa Catalina to **Parque San Telmo**, and walk south along Calle Mayor de Triana. Cross a major highway and you reach **Vegueta**, the oldest part of the city, where Spanish forces

Playing on Gran Canaria's pristine Maspalomas dunes *(see page 63)*

first set up camp in 1478. A district of narrow, pretty streets, it centres on **Plaza de Sant Ana**, home of the **Catedral de Santa Ana** (open Mon–Sat, Sat am only; admission fee includes the museum) and the adjoining **Museo Diocesano de Arte Sacro**. Close by is the lovely 15th-century **Casa de Colón** (open daily, weekends am only; admission fee). Columbus is said to have stayed here, before setting off on his 1492 voyage, but there is no evidence to support this. Now an atmospheric museum with a pretty courtyard, it recreates the Age of Discovery with exhibits of navigational instruments, charts and weapons. Not far away, the **Museo Canario** (open daily, weekends am only; admission fee) holds the Canary Islands' most important collection of pre-Hispanic objects, including a room full of Cro-Magnon skulls and mummies.

Located to the north of the city (it's best to get a bus or taxi back past Parque Santa Catalina) is the lovely Playa de las

The Casa de Colón, one of Las Palmas' most splendid sites

Canteras, a 3km (2-mile) stretch of sand, with shallow waters, lots of restaurants, and a good, local atmosphere, as it is frequented mostly by locals from Las Palmas and visitors from the Spanish mainland.

Excursions from Las Palmas
If you prefer to explore independently of the shore excursions offered by the cruise line, buses run regu-

The Plaza Teresa de Bolívar in Teror is a peaceful spot

larly from the port-side terminal (or another in Parque San Telmo) to most parts of the island – but leave plenty of time to get back. Or gang together in a group of four or more and negotiate a private tour by taxi; given sufficient numbers, this can work out a lot cheaper than the ships' excursions, but do double-check timings and establish a set rate in advance.

Playa del Inglés in the south (journey time about 50 minutes) is crammed with high-rise hotels, fast-food joints and amusements of all kinds; it is not to everyone's taste, but the beaches are wonderful. The resort adjoins the glorious **Maspalomas** sand dunes, now a nature reserve. The next major resort is **Puerto Rico** to the west. It is lively, family-orientated and has the best watersports facilities on the island. A little further on is the pretty harbour of Puerto de Mogán, with streets built over a series of little canals.

Teror, 22km (14 miles) inland from Las Palmas and served by frequent buses, is a country town famous for the intricately carved wooden balconies of its splendid houses (one of which can be visited), and the **Basílica de Nuestra Señora del Pino**, which commemorates a vision of the

Barranco de Guayadeque

Virgin Mary in the branches of a pine tree, seen by shepherds in 1481. The journey there is lovely.

The bus or taxi ride to **Arucas**, the island's banana capital, situated to the west of Las Palmas, ascends into the mountains. The old part of town has atmospheric winding cobbled streets, and is overshadowed by the huge, neo-Gothic lava-stone church of **San Juan Bautista**. Both Teror and Arucas can be visited on an excursion, as can the lush gorge of **Barranco de Guayadeque**, where there are inhabited cave dwellings.

Lanzarote

Lanzarote has one of the most attractive climates in the world, and is worth exploring for its spectacular moon-like volcanic landscape (cataclysmic eruptions in the 1730s and the 1820s smothered the island in lava, creating its weird, other-worldly terrain). The island has 300 volcanoes and has been designated a world biosphere reserve by UNESCO. Beach lovers can soak up the sun and enjoy the colourful volcanic sand beaches (red, white or black); or you can visit some of the buildings and monuments created by the Canary Islands' most famous artist and architect, César Manrique.

⚓ **Arrecife** is Lanzarote's main port, and cruise ships berth among the cargo docks at Muelle de los Marmoles; a small terminal nearby serves both cruise ship and ferry passengers with toilets, telephones and taxis, and shuttle services operate into the town centre, a 30-minute walk away. There are plans to redesign Muelle de los Marmoles exclusively for cruise calls, moving freight operations to other docks.

Arrecife's centre is compact and has shops and restaurants centred around the waterfront avenues Generalísimo Franco and León y Castillo. There is also a decent beach but, while pleasant enough, the town doesn't justify a long stay, although you might want to visit the **Castillo de San José**, a few kilometres north of the centre, a well-preserved fortress that houses a small but impressive **Museo de Arte Contemporáneo**. If you want to see more of the island and are not taking one of the ship's excursions, go inland to the bus station in Via Medular, or get a cab at the rank near the port.

Windmill and cacti on the Lanzarote landscape

At **Tahiche**, just 12km (7 miles) away, pay a visit to the **Fundación César Manrique** (open Mon–Sat; admission fee), dedicated to the artist. It's based in his house, built on the lava fields and has subterranean chambers created by air bubbles in the lava flow. Manrique's influence can also be seen in the **Jardín de Cactus** (open daily; admission fee) at **Guatiza**, about 9km (5 miles) north of Tahiche, where there are more than 1,500 varieties of cacti. Another 10km (6 miles) will get you to the

Manrique-designed volcanic caves of **Jameos del Agua** (open daily; admission fee). There is a saltwater lagoon inhabited by tiny blind albino crabs, unique to the island, and ethereal mood music accompanies your descent into the cave. You need to be fairly fit, though, as the approach involves walking up 150 steps. The spectacular **Cueva de los Verdes** is part of the complex.

Whatever else you do, try to visit the **Parque Nacional de Timanfaya** (open daily; admission fee), which encompasses the area known as Montañas de Fuego (Mountains of Fire) with their fantastical shapes created by solidified volcanic lava. This is an active volcanic area, and a guide will demonstrate it by pouring water down a tube into the earth, whereupon a geyser of hot water erupts. The point is also made in a nearby restaurant, where meat is grilled on heat rising directly from the ground. Just outside the park, at **Echadero de los Camellos**, you can take a camel ride up the volcanic slopes.

La Palma

It has two nicknames – La Isla Bonita (The Beautiful Island) and La Isla Verde (The Green Island) and both are appropriate. Its statistics are impressive, too. The highest peak, Roque de los Muchachos, rises 2,423m (7,950ft) above sea level, making it the steepest island in the world in relation to its total area. It is also the only one of the Canary Islands to have even very small streams.

⚓ **Santa Cruz de la Palma**, the island capital, is an appealing town – clean and bright with traditional and modern architecture side-by-side creating a pleasing atmosphere. Most people agree that it is the most attractive of the Canary Islands' capitals. Northern tours from cruise ships are likely to visit **Mirador de San Bartolomé** and the Los Tilos evergreen forest, while those to the south often visit the sanctuary of **Las Nieves**, the **Caldera de Taburiente** and the **Teneguia volcano**.

The Rock of Gibraltar

GIBRALTAR

The British seized **Gibraltar** from Spain in 1704 and, despite the Great Siege of 1779–83, when the Spanish tried to retake it, it has remained in British hands ever since. It is a popular port of call with cruise passengers because it offers tax-free shopping and a wide range of experiences in a short time. Because it is so easily explorable, ships are not bound to spend a full day here. Note that customs regulations forbid cruise passengers visiting Gibraltar from going over the border into Spain.

Gibraltar's main centre is an easy 2km (1-mile) walk up a straight road from the port. You can also take a shuttle service or taxi into town. Gibraltar's Main Street and its adjoining lanes and byways offer plenty of shops, pubs and cafés.

Attractions on the Rock include **St Michael's Cave** (open daily 9.30am–7pm; admission fee), an imposing natural phenomenon with an upper hall linked by subterranean passages to a lower cave that leads on to other chambers, 82m (250ft)

A cheeky Barbary ape

below the surface, with an underground lake. The upper hall is often used as an auditorium for concerts. The cave's stalagmites and stalactites make an impressive backdrop for twice-daily *son-et-lumière* shows.

The walled **Moorish Castle**, believed to date from the 8th century, is another highlight, not least for its Tower of Homage, which has survived 14 sieges, and the 48km (30-mile) **Upper Galleries** (tower and galleries open daily 9.30am–7pm; admission fee), tunnels dug by the British when the rock was surrounded by Spanish and French forces in 1779. Inside the fortified walls of the castle you can see a daily Changing of the Guard. The castle complex is also well known for its range of English pubs.

The **Gibraltar Museum** (open Mon–Fri 10am–6pm, Sat 10am–2pm; admission fee), built over a 14th-century Moorish bath house, tells the Rock's story from prehistoric times, focusing on the Battle of Trafalgar (1805). Admiral Nelson's ship, the *Victory*, carrying his body, preserved in brandy, stopped at the Rock for repairs en route to England. Many of the Trafalgar dead are buried on Gibraltar, although the **Trafalgar Cemetery** was, in fact, operational from 1708 to 1835 and used for the burial of English seamen who died from wounds at three naval battles besides Trafalgar.

Gibraltar is famed for its Barbary apes – the only apes still living wild in Europe; there are about 160 of them, some living in the **Apes' Den** (open daily 9.30am–7pm; admission fee). According to tradition, Britain will lose Gibraltar only when the apes no longer live there. During World War II, when numbers were diminishing, the army built the den to encourage the animals to breed and bolster morale. Other apes live in the area surrounding the Great Siege tunnels. Look out for black-furred babies but do not approach them – and beware if you see an ape pouting at you, as this is a warning to keep your distance.

A cable car runs from the Grand Parade up to the Rock Restaurant with magnificent views across Algeciras Bay and the Strait to Morocco's Rif Mountains. Halfway up, it drops visitors off to see the apes. At the top, multi-lingual tapes can be hired to give you an overview of Gibraltar's history.

Gibraltar has over 300 days of sunshine a year, and there are several beaches on which you can make the most of it. Eastern Beach is the largest, but by far the prettiest is **Catalan Bay**, which has fishing boats and good seafood restaurants where you can have a pleasant lunch.

Sailing the Strait of Gibraltar

Ships entering the Mediterranean from the the Atlantic pass through the choppy Strait of Gibraltar, the narrow channel, 13km (8 miles) wide, that separates Europe from Africa, and the Atlantic from the Mediterranean. Try to be on deck as the ship comes into the strait, where the water is the feeding ground for schools of dolphins and sperm whales. As you head in from the Atlantic, the limestone Rock of Gibraltar is on the port (left) side. The Romans believed this to be one of the two Pillars of Hercules, the second of which, Jebel Musa, is visible to starboard, in Morocco. The strait is the only point at which water from the Atlantic can flow into the Mediterranean basin. The depth and narrowness of the channel and the speed at which water flows through it means that violent winds can often blow up unexpectedly.

Migratory birds pass over the strait, and from March to May and August to October, honey buzzards, black kites, storks, griffon vultures, short-toed eagles, ospreys, buzzards and sparrowhawks can be seen.

France

Climate Summer temperatures can climb to as high as 40°C (104°F), often followed by heavy thunderstorms. November enjoys a little sunshine, but from December the Mediterranean often has long periods of clear blue skies.

Time Zone For most of the year, the time in France is GMT+1.

Opening Times Banks are normally open from 9am–noon and 2–5pm Monday–Friday. Most shops open at 9/10am, and nearly all stores close for a long lunch from noon–2/3pm. The majority of shops shut daily at 7pm.

What to Buy The great joy of France is its food, and the markets are the best places to appreciate the quality of ingredients and buy transportable staples. Besides food markets, most large towns have second-hand and flea markets. The vitality and interest of town and city centres have been consciously preserved through a preference for small and individual shops.

Money Matters Euro.

Public Holidays 1 January, Easter Monday, Labour Day (1 May), Ascension Day, 8 May, Whit Monday, 14 July, 15 August, 1, 11 November and 25 December.

Etiquette French manners call for the use of 'Monsieur', 'Madame' and 'Mademoiselle' in nearly all situations.

Tipping Restaurant bills usually include service (*service compris)* and taxi drivers are customarily given a 10 percent tip.

Hazards and Security The usual precautions should be taken, especially in poorly lit dock areas at night.

Drugs and Medicines French chemists have wider prescribing powers than those in the UK or US, so it is sometimes worth going to a pharmacy rather than a doctor. Medical standards in France are high, but a *feuille des soins* will be necessary to obtain a refund under EU agreements.

Emergency Telephone Numbers Police 17; ambulance 15; fire 18.

The boulangerie: a staple of French life

FRANCE

A cruise-line itinerary that takes in the ports of southern France and Corsica will whisk you into the edgy, exciting atmosphere of Marseille, the sophistication and heady Mediterranean scents of cities such as Cannes and Nice, the glitz of St-Tropez and the anomaly that is the independent protectorate of Monaco. There are quieter places too, such as pretty Villefranche, which inspired Jean Cocteau. And there are several ports of call on the island of Corsica, which, though wild, rugged and seemingly a different world from the Riviera ports, is still essentially very French in character.

Marseille

Founded as Massalia in the 6th century BC by Greeks from Phocaea on the coast of Asia Minor, **Marseille** has been a significant Mediterranean port ever since. As well as being a premier port for southern Europe and Africa, it was the place where Louis XIV moored his huge fleet. During the revolution, Marseille gave France her national anthem, *La Marseillaise*.

Yet, like many working ports, it suffers from a bad reputation. Although often referred to as 'the crime capital of the Mediterranean', investment and a more rigorous civic attitude have helped clean up the city's act, and many of the older buildings have been scrubbed and renovated.

The first view of Marseille gives a taste of its rough glamour, with modern high-rise flats under brown and white hills and a tangle of dockside cranes. Cruise ships normally dock in Marseille for a full day. In the terminus, about 15–20 minutes' drive from the harbour front, there is a bar and a range of shops. Shuttle buses (and taxis) link the dock to the **Vieux Port** (Old Port). A blue-and-white, open-sided **Petit Train de Vieux** then leaves every 20 minutes from the quai du Port, close to where the shuttle buses drop off passengers. Trains take sightseers on two routes; a one-hour tour to the cathedral or a 40-minute tour of the old town, known as the Panier Quarter.

The pretty **Hôtel de Ville** (Town Hall), built in 1653, looks onto the harbour. Flags of the *tricolore* hang at the front above ornate ironwork and huge windows.

The main boulevard from the old port is **La Canebière**, Marseille's main street. A lovely *belle époque* carousel immediately sets a distinctly French tone. On the right of the street is the bright, modern **Office du Tourisme**, which sells good-value *Carte Privilèges*, giving a day's entry to many of the museums. Among the cafés and perfume shops on La Canebière are the **Maritime Museum** (open Wed–Mon 10am–noon, 2–6pm; admission fee), and fashion museum,

> From Marseille harbour you can take a short ferry to Château d'If, the setting for the novel *The Count of Monte Cristo*, or to Îles du Frioul, with crystal blue lagoons that are great for swimming.

Sailing around the old Phocaean port of Marseille

the **Musée de la Mode** (open Tues–Sun noon–7pm; admission fee). Dwarf palm trees nestle among the street lamps on the busy boulevard. Off La Canebière, a right turn leads into rue Longues des Capucins, where there is an Arab street market selling spicy foods and trinkets.

A taxi or metro ride (Métro Cinq-Avenues) takes you to the **Palais Longchamp** (avenue Longchamp) in place Bernex, a semicircular colonnade looking out over fountains in formal grounds. The Palais was built in 1838 as the city's water tower. The building also houses the **Musée de Beaux-Arts** and the **Musée d'Histoire Naturelle** (both open Tues–Sun 11am–6pm in summer, 10am–5pm in winter; admission fee).

Looking like a ramshackle ancient village, **Le Panier** gives an impression of old Marseille. Beginning just behind the Hôtel de Ville are the steep streets and steps up the hill, past tree-shaded restaurants, modern fountains and three- to five-storey buildings with balconies and handsome shutters.

In place de la Major is the **Cathédrale de la Major**. High on the hill above the bay, the **Basilique-de-Notre-Dame-de-la-Garde** is worth visiting, not least for the view from its distinctive tower, a local landmark. Bus No. 60 goes from Cours Ballard, or you can take a metro to Joliette.

In addition to the half-day tours devoted to shopping and 'panoramic' Marseille, you may be offered full-day excursions to Avignon, Aix-en-Provence and Les Baux.

Avignon

'Honey-coloured, rose-faded walls', was how the novelist Lawrence Durrell described the mighty ramparts of **Avignon**. Built in the 14th century on the orders of the popes, the walls encircle the old city for a distance of 4km (2½ miles). With so many attractions to choose from in this historic city, you might just want to opt out and go for a stroll

Performing in front of the Palais des Papes, Avignon

along the stretch of walls that follows the banks of the Rhône. Here, you will find yourself lingering over views of the picturesque **Pont St-Bénezet**, the famous bridge on which, according to the song, *on y danse*. Once 22 arches strode across the river, but most were swept away in the floods of 1668, though the lovely Gothic chapel on the cobbled bridge was spared. A little further on you can descend the ramparts to explore the **Rocher des Doms**, from whose gardens you can survey the city's papal palaces and churches in one great sweep.

If you're more inclined to explore the sights, then make your way to the **Palais des Papes**, the huge fortress that the popes built as their base in the city during the 14th century. Some guided tours take in the splendid apartments and halls, decorated with frescoes and tapestries, where popes once slept, held audiences and hosted grand banquets.

Aix-en-Provence

The capital of Provence, **Aix** is a town of lavish Renaissance architecture, host to a huge market that fills the streets on Tuesdays, Thursdays and Saturdays. The compact Old Town is focused on cours Mirabeau, a café-lined avenue that is at the heart of local life. The rows of plane trees that march down this avenue form a green arbour to shade shoppers browsing the bookshops or admiring the balconied facades of gracious 17th-century mansions. Four fountains add to the charm of the scene; the **Fontaine d'Eau Thermeau** still pours out naturally hot water from the spring that first put Aix on the map as a Roman spa. Walk north a short way from cours Mirabeau and you will find the **Musée de Vieil Aix**, hidden among a tangle of narrow lanes, covering local history and folklore. Nearby is the cathedral, **St-Sauveur**, built on the site of the Roman Forum, with a 5th-century baptistery.

South of cours Mirabeau is the **Mazarin quarter**, an area of aristocratic mansions, where the **Musée Granet** exhibits archaeological finds, and paintings by Cézanne. The artist was born in Aix in 1839, and his distinctive style was developed as he painted local landmarks, such as the Mont Ste-Victoire that dominates the Aix countryside.

Les Baux

This part of Provence is particularly renowned for lavender products – toiletries, scented pillows and perfume.

Due south of Avignon, **Les Baux** is set on the stony heights of the Alpilles, the last chain of high peaks before Provence descends to the marshy Camargues and then to the sea. The roads to the village climbs through herb-and-pine-scented *garrigues*, the wild vegetation of these jagged and barren rocks. Down below the monastic hospital at **St-Rémy** where Van Gogh sought asylum after cutting off part of his ear.

Up above, in the 'modern' village of Baux, there are scores of shops selling local crafts and Provençal ceramics. Higher still, the so-called **Ville Mort** (Dead City) is an eerie place of ruined rock-cut houses and lofty views that stretch to the peaks of the surrounding hills. Back at the foot of the village, look out for the former bauxite quarry (the mineral bauxite gets its name from Les Baux) fancifully renamed the Cathédrale des Images, and the equally evocative **Val d'Enfer** (Hell Valley), a chaotic rock-strewn gorge.

St-Tropez

It is hard to imagine now, but in Roman times **St-Tropez** was a place of Christian pilgrimage. Much later, the patronage of writers such as Guy de Maupassant and artists including Paul Signac and Henri Matisse made this once-sleepy fishing village a fashionable place to visit. And after the literati came the glitterati, with Roger Vadim making *And God Created Woman* in 1956, turning both Brigitte Bardot and St-Tropez into movie stars. It is now a magnet for the rich and famous – Bardot, Elton John and Mick Jagger have all owned villas here.

St-Tropez – like Cannes – is particularly favoured by the smaller, luxury ships, which tend to stay late into the evening to allow passengers to enjoy the lively nightlife.

Dining on a sultry St-Tropez night

The small dock area is designed for private yachts, not cruise ships, so cruise visitors are tendered in to either the Vieux Port or Nouveau Port (old and new ports) but, as these are just 150m/yds apart, there is little chance of confusion. From the new port, you walk straight past the old one into the town. There are no terminals but there is a tourist information centre near each landing stage (the main one is on quai Jean Jaurès, by the old port).

Surrounding the port is a host of cafés, restaurants and shops, which sell mainly nautical items to the yachties who can walk into the shops straight off their floating gin palaces. There are taxis along quai Jean Jaurès but, unless you want to go out of the resort, it is much easier and quicker to walk around it. The principal shopping street – rue François Sibilli – links the old port and the town's main squares.

One of the most popular attractions, the **Musée de l'Annonciade** (open Wed–Mon Jun–Sept 10am–noon, 3–7pm, Oct–May 10am–noon, 2–6pm; admission fee), a 16th-century chapel-turned-art museum, features original works by Signac, Bonnard, Dufy and their contemporaries. It is located between the ports on place Grammont, quai Gabriel Peri. From quai Jean Jaurès by the old port, turn sharp left and there is a long promontory lined with cafés and restaurants with superb views of the Gulf of St-Tropez. Alternatively, head directly inland and you are in the old town – a maelstrom of designer boutiques, cafés and restaurants along every street and alleyway.

In July and August, walking tours are organised from the tourist office but it is easy to tour independently. The town church, the Église de St-Tropez, is right in the centre, but the main icon is the 16th-century **Citadelle**, a fort on a hill overlooking the old town. This is walkable from the dock and, although some effort is required to reach it, the view across St-Tropez and its bay is spectacular. There is a maritime museum, **Musée Naval** (open Wed–Sun Jun–Sept 10am–noon, 2–7pm, Oct–May 10am–noon, 2–5pm; admission fee) in the dungeon.

There are public beaches (Graniers) just below the citadelle and by the fishing harbour (Port des Pecheurs) but the better (private) beaches are past the headland, at least 3km (2 miles) away on an 8-km (5-mile) stretch of sand called Pampelonne. To reach them, either take a taxi (expensive) or one of the frequent beach shuttle mini-buses (from place des Lices on boulevard Vasserpt, a 10- to 15-minute walk to the right of the old port). But, especially in midsummer, expect a frustrating start to the journey in the seemingly permanent traffic jams.

There are fees to use the beaches, on which topless and – on a couple of them – bottomless sunbathing is the norm.

Most cruise lines offer excursions to nearby **Ramatuelle** and **Gassin**, pretty hilltop villages surrounded by vineyards and windmills. **Port Grimaud**, 10km (6 miles) away, is a picturesque town built in the 1960s over a series of waterways; while Grimaud itself is a medieval town with a ruined château.

Cannes

Discovered by the British in the 1830s, **Cannes** now bears little resemblance to the fishing village it once was, and is arguably the grandest of all the French Riviera resorts. It is swisher than Nice, more glamorous than Villefranche and – thanks to the media circus of its film festival every May– perhaps even more famous than St-Tropez. Set in the Bay of Cannes, it is a convenient gateway to the Côte d'Azur with good transport links to other Riviera resorts.

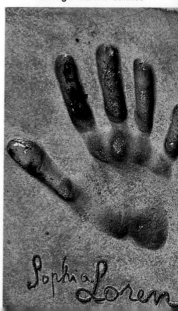

Making a mark in Cannes

Cannes is occasionally used as a home port by lines with smaller ships – luxury five-star or sail-cruisers – and home-porting ships usually depart early evening. Visiting ships have to anchor off and tender passengers into a small quay, which also handles local ferries; they often stay until late evening, allowing passengers to experience

When shopping in Cannes, as well as perfume from nearby Grasse, look out for uniquely designed glass-ware from the glass-works at Biot, a village 12km (7 miles) away.

the renowned Riviera night-life. (The quay is at the far corner of a busy square with colourful market stalls that stretch in front of a line of open-air cafés and restau-rants, making this a lovely place to dine in the evening.)

Turn left outside the ter-minal and immediately left again and you are in the market square, which has a bus terminal at the far end. The railway station is a five-minute walk in the other direction (behind the Palais des Festivals and the town's main drag, boulevard de la Croisette).

Cannes is easily explored on foot. Just west of the Vieux Port is the oldest part of town, **Le Suquet**, an area of narrow streets full of attractive shops and cafés, with a medieval church, Nôtre-Dame de l'Espérance, and a 12th-century castle, which houses the **Musée de la Castre** (open all year, hours vary; admission fee) with interesting ethnographic and archae-ological collections. But the major draw is in the opposite di-rection: the palm tree-lined **boulevard de la Croisette** which stretches eastwards from the Palais des Festivals (venue for the Cannes Film Festival in May) opposite the terminal, and along the seafront to the other end of the bay. This is where the action is: the swish hotels, smart casinos, stylish boutiques, discreet art galleries and marinas packed with lavishly fitted yachts. Lunch at any of the many cafés and restaurants is an expensive business but it is worth pausing for a drink just to watch the beautiful people that Cannes continues to attract.

For a different view of Cannes, head for the **Observatoire** (Observatory) of Super-Cannes, a suburb north of the rail-way station. This has lifts up to viewing platforms overlook-ing Cannes and the coastline.

Nice and Villefranche-sur-Mer

Nice and Villefranche are just 5km (3 miles) apart but, while Nice is a major resort with many grand hotels, wide avenues full of department stores, large squares, historic churches and several major museums, Villefranche remains a small, relatively uncrowded town with plenty of Gallic charm but no major historical attractions. For the cruise visitor, though, either place is a genuine attraction in its own right and the two ports are so close together that shore excursions are identical from both.

Nice will sometimes be substituted for Villefranche, which has deep water, if sea conditions rule out tendering passengers ashore – hence the two ports being grouped together here. For both, though, a full-day stay is the norm, with the occasional ship extending its time in Nice until about 11pm.

Hôtel Negresco, long a Nice landmark

Nice

At **Nice**, the port area (Lympia) is at the eastern end of the bay. Cruise ships currently dock in a small basin where ferries also embark, but there are plans for a new cruise ship-only dock with a purpose-built terminal. When that is built, more ships will home-port in Nice but at present there are few facilities in the dock area (although there are many bars and bistros nearby). It is,

> **Explaining why he loved Nice so much, the painter Henri Matisse (1869–1954) wrote: 'When I understood that, every morning, I would see that light, I could not believe my good fortune.'**

however, only around a 20-minute walk westward, around quai Rauba Capeu, along quai des États-Unis and past Nice's original main promenade (Les Ponchettes), to the most interesting part of Nice – the old town (Vieux Nice) – and not much further to the lengthy Promenades des Anglais, lined with splendid *belle époque* mansions and hotels, and overlooking a series of 13 fee-charging beaches. Between the port and the old town, there is also a worthwhile detour up 400 steps to the beautiful gardens of **Le Château**.

The mixture of colourfully painted houses, narrow streets, cafés and restaurants makes **Vieux Nice** the most attractive part of the city, and the most walkable. Worth a visit are the 17th-century **Cathédrale Ste-Réparate**, the 18th-century baroque **Chapelle de la Miséricorde**, and the splendid **Palais Lascaris** (open Tues–Sun 10am–12pm, 2–6pm; free).

One of the greatest attractions, is the huge, colourful fish, flower and vegetable market on **cours Saleya**, held every morning except Monday, when there is an antiques market.

If you have time, include the **Musée d'Art Contemptorain** (promenade des Arts), **Musée Nationale Marc Chagall** (avenue du Docteur Ménard) and **Musée Matisse** (164 avenue des Arénes de Cimiez) on your itinerary (open Wed–Mon, except Musée d'Art, which is open Tues–Sun; all 10am–6pm; admission fee). The first is easily walkable, northeast along rue Jean Jaurès; there are buses to the others, but they're best reached by taxi if time is limited. Though extremely interesting, neither is too large and will not detain you overlong.

This is a good city for shoppers. Avenue Jean Médecin has a range of stores and a US-style mall, while cours Julien, at the top of La Canebière will tempt those looking for French fashions. The streets around cours Saleya *(see opposite)* are home to a number of interesting old shops selling typical products of the region, such as good-quality olive oil, oil-based soaps and lavender products. It's also a good place to buy locally made perfume – there is one perfume factory in nearby Eze *(see page 85)* and numerous other major houses in the perfume capital, Grasse *(see page 86)*.

In order to appreciate the true Niçoise atmosphere, the best places to eat are in Vieux Nice, especially around cours Saleya. Choose from upmarket fish restaurants or down-to-earth spots selling *socca*, the local version of pizza, made of roasted chickpeas, and *salade niçoise*. The area around the Vieux Port is the place for *bouillabaisse*, a rich fish stew that is a local speciality.

Villefranche-sur-Mer

Villefranche-sur-Mer

Tenders bring you into a small jetty at the western end of **Villefranche-sur-Mer**. The centre of Ville-franche is just behind the terminal, across the road and up a series of steps. Alternatively, turn right to walk along the seafront to a long, narrow beach which curls around the east of the bay.

Despite the fact that so many ships call at Villefranche, it is a quiet, relaxed place. This is partly because so many passengers take a tour or travel independently to the neighbouring Riviera resorts, but also because the area between the seafront road and the upper road (part of the Lower Corniche), is a succession of narrow pedestrianised streets, steps and alleyways with shuttered houses painted in pastel shades. Here, and along the seafront, are many cafés, restaurants and *pâtisseries*.

The main place to visit is the **Chapelle de St-Pierre**, a tiny fishermen's chapel, its interior decorated by the writer and artist Jean Cocteau (1889–1963), who loved Villefranche.

It's easy to reach Nice and Monaco from Villefranche by train, though there are taxis outside the terminal if your budget allows. The station is under 10 minutes' walk from the terminal, at the top of steps opposite where the beach begins – look out for a French railways (SNCF) sign on the wall, as the steps are partially obscured from the promenade. There are usually two or three trains an hour; Nice is just 7 minutes away, Cannes 25 minutes, and Monaco, less than 20 minutes.

Excursions from Nice and Villefranche

Excursions from Nice and Villefranche include half-day tours to the hilltop village of Eze, the artists' haunt of St-

Paul-de-Vence or the perfume town of Grasse. Whole days in Cannes and Monaco are also usually tour options.

Eze is perched on a rocky spike that pokes high above the sea, to the west of Villefranche. Built here to deter invaders, the village now attracts them instead – thanks to its romantic narrow lanes, stone staircases and pretty old houses. The best viewpoint in the village is the Jardin Exotique, which surrounds the ruined fortress at a height of 429m (1,407ft) above sea level. On a clear day, it is claimed that you can see all the way to Corsica. From Eze, an old mule track plunges down to the seaside town of Eze-Bord-de-Mer, sister to the hilltop

Eze, a classic Riviera *village perché*

town. The footpath is called sentier de Nietzsche, after the German romantic philosopher who often walked along it.

The walled town of **St-Paul-de-Vence** was constructed by François I in the 16th century as a defence against Nice and the dukes of Savoy. Although the town is pretty in its own right – a tour of the narrow pedestrian streets takes only a few minutes – art is the big pull here. The Colombe d'Or hotel, across the street from the main square, place du Général de Gaulle, has an important private collection of modern art, acquired from Picasso, Léger and Calder, in exchange for meals in the restaurant. And the **Fondation Maeght** (open daily Oct–Jun 10am–12.30pm and 2–6pm, July–Sept 10am–7pm; admission fee), a museum set on a wooded hill just outside town, displays works by Chagall, Miró, Braque and other modern masters.

Grasse is a pretty inland town where you can visit the Musée International de la Parfumerie and the Fragonard Parfumerie, both of which run tours and show how scents are made. You can, of course, buy perfume, and visit the house where the painter Jean-Honoré Fragonard was born in 1732.

Monaco

For a place less than 5 sq km (2 sq miles) in size, the Principality of **Monaco** attracts a lot of attention. It is glitz and glamour all the way, starting with a harbour where some of the lavishly appointed yachts have never seen the open sea, their owners preferring to tie-up permanently at one of the world's chicest addresses. On the three land sides of the harbour are Monaco's three main districts: Monaco Ville (the old town), La Condamine (the commercial and residential area overlooking the harbour) and Monte-Carlo (the new town). Walking or being driven around the steep, winding, narrow streets that link these districts, it is hard to imagine drivers negotiating the same bends at 160kph (100mph) plus, when the Grand Prix circus comes to town every year. Many of the

The Principality of Monaco

street names also remind you of the mixture of history and Hollywood that has been part of the Grimaldi family that still rules the Principality. In 1297, François Grimaldi captured the fortress at Monaco, and his family bought the surrounding area from Genoa 11 years later. The principality made the headlines in 1955 when Prince Rainier III married film star Grace Kelly; she was killed in a car crash on the Corniche in 1982. By the time Rainier died in 2005, he had become Europe's longest-reigning monarch. His son, Prince Albert, is the current ruler. Still independent (although a French protectorate), Monaco continues to thrive on a mixture of manufacturing, financial services, tourism and gambling revenues.

For passengers to avail themselves of the lively nightlife, ships tend to arrive in the morning and leave late in the evening. The largest ships still have to anchor off the port but smaller ones pull in alongside on a new floating dock on the ocean side of the inner harbour, close to La Condamine.

If your budget allows, Monaco is a good place to buy designer fashions. The main stores are in Monte-Carlo (boulevard des Moulins and avenues des Beaux-Arts and Princess Grace), but there are also boutiques in La Condamine (rues Grimaldi and Caroline). Should you be interested, Princess Stephanie has her own swimwear label.

From the new dock, Monaco Ville sits up on the hill to the left, while Monte-Carlo is up on the headland to the right (via La Condamine). Either is walkable from the ship with a lift at the east end of Rampe Major (from quai Antoine) to avoid negotiating the steep hill that leads up to Monaco Ville.

Highlights of Monaco Ville include the elaborate Changing of the Guard (daily 11.55am) at the Palais du Prince; the tomb of Princess Grace in the Byzantine-style Cathédrale St-Nicolas; and several museums, of which the pick is the state-of-the-art sealife centre, the **Musée Océanographique** (open daily Jan–Mar 10am–6pm, Apr–Jun and Sept 9.30am–7pm, Jul–Aug 9.30am–7.30pm; admission fee). A tourist train starts and finishes tours of Monaco Ville from outside this museum.

The star of Monte-Carlo is the **Grand Casino** (dress code, admission fee and passports necessary for entry), Europe's first when opened in 1856. Along with the Opera House, it stands in place du Casino on the headland looking at the harbour. Lifts to the upper levels of La Condamine are a shortcut to the station (boulevard Rainier III) and the **Jardin Exotique** (open daily mid-May–mid-Sept 9am–7pm, mid-Sept–mid-May 9am–6pm; admission fee), home to sub-tropical plants.

Half-day tours from Monaco typically go to St Paul-de-Vence, Antibes and Eze; full days are usually offered to Nice, Cannes and Grasse. Frequent trains to Eze, Villefranche-sur-Mer, Nice, Juan-les-Pins and Cannes are alternatives to the organised tours.

Corsica

Lying 160km (100 miles) southwest of the French Riviera and 80km (50 miles) west of the coast of Italy, **Corsica** has been described as the 'Scented Isle' because of the fragrance of its *maquis* – the low-level layer of evergreen herbs, plants and flowers among its sometimes densely wooded interior – but Corsica's appeal really lies in its majestic scenery, with spectacular mountains in the interior and some superb coastline. Many of the old port towns, notably Bonifacio and Calvi, are extremely picturesque.

The independently minded people have fought many battles over the centuries, and the island did not become part of France until 1768 (the year before its favourite son, Napoleon Bonaparte, was born in Ajaccio), when it was ceded from Genoa. The islanders retain a strong sense of identity to this day.

Views over the Corsican landscape, peppered with scented *maquis*

Ajaccio

⚓ Set in a fine, wide bay, **Ajaccio** has intermittently been the capital of Corsica since it was founded by the Genoese in 1492. The city itself is a fascinating mixture of old and new and basks in its strong Napoleonic connections. Ships usually stay a full day.

The port is towards the northern end of the bay, and, although there is much modern building in the city, the historic citadel overlooking it creates an impressive approach. Most ships dock rather than tender passengers ashore.

Most excursions start with a tour around Ajaccio itself but this is easily accomplished independently. The main market place (selling handicrafts as well as food) is within sight of the pier. The Vieille Ville (Old Town), located below the citadel, is home to the **Maison Napoleon** (open Mon 2pm–6pm, Tues–Sat 9am–12am, 2pm–6pm; admission fee); the cathedral, where the great leader was baptised, is just a short walk from there. The main shopping street – cours Napoleon – borders the old town. In the newer part of the city, there are wide, tree-lined boulevards, parks and squares, and, predictably, numerous statues of Napoleon.

One of the many Corsican tributes to local lad, Napoleon

Trips from Ajaccio: There are beaches within the city limits (the best is down the steps from boulevard Lantivy), boat trips to the pretty **Iles Sanguinaires** just offshore in the bay, and plenty of taxis to take you further inland – at a high price, however. There is also a railway station, from where there are regular scenic, if slow-moving, services to **Corte**, the original island capital.

The villages of Cargese, Pinto and Filitosa, the Calanches de Piana, and the Spelunca Gorges are on the usual full-day tour from Ajaccio, while half-day trips may visit the Prunella Gorges and Lake Tolla.

Calvi

Very much a resort town now, **Calvi** is an attractive destination as well as being close enough for excursions to some of Corsica's best-known or most historic attractions. Like Ajaccio and Bonifacio, the first impression when approaching this

Spectacular mountains rise above Corte, a day trip from Ajaccio

Corsican port is the imposing presence of a huge citadel overlooking the town. Quai Landry is attractively landscaped and has many pleasant cafés overlooking the waterfront, but it lies on a busy road, behind which lies the centre of the resort's vibrant nightlife. Ships have to anchor off and tender into the port area. Stays are either a full or half day.

Within Calvi, as in many Mediterranean ports, there are two levels: the new town down by the port and an older quarter up towards the citadel. These are best explored on foot, with the **Cathédrale St-Jean Baptiste** and the **Oratoire St-Antoine** the most impressive buildings along the way to the huge 15th-century **Citadelle**. To explore outside

Corsican Coast

The Mediterranean's 4th largest island, Corsica has 1,000km (620 miles) of coastline, with beaches of fine golden sand and rocky bays, as shown above, at the Golfe de Porto, south of Calvi. Inland, granite peaks climb to 2,710m (8,900ft), giving Corsica the nickname 'mountain in the sea'.

Calvi independently, there are (costly) taxis, locally booked coach excursions, or a train service either inland or, notably, to the lively resort of **L'Ille Rousse** situated further up the west coast.

Bonifacio

On the southern tip of the island is Corsica's second city, **Bonifacio**. The harbour affords excellent views of the towering cliffs that surround it, and the city itself is full of historic interest. Cruise ships usually stay a full day here. Most ships have to anchor off and tender passengers in.

The arrival into Bonifacio is one of the most impressive in Mediterranean cruising. Turning from the sea into the Goulet de Bonifacio, the sheltered inlet, it is easy to imagine the days when the port was a pirate stronghold. Surrounded by white chalk cliffs and overlooked by the medieval citadel, even the compact Bonifacio townhouses are designed fortress-style to withstand sieges. Nowadays, of course, the only invasion is by passengers from visiting cruise ships and the only pirates the ones who own the smart cafés, restaurants and souvenir shops that line the quayside and charge inflated French Riviera-style prices.

The lower level of the town centre is right behind the quay. There is no need to take an organised tour of Bonifacio itself, as it's easy to explore independently; however, a boat trip around the inlet does offer the best views of the ancient houses perched precariously on the cliffside and is the only way of exploring the cave of **Sdragonato**, which has a hole in its ceiling that is shaped just like Corsica.

It is, though, a steep walk up the rock face, via the rough-hewn 15th-century 'King of Aragon's Staircase', or a much longer walk by road up to the 13th-century **Citadelle** and **Haute Ville** (Upper Town). The huge walls of the citadel jut out over the chalk cliff, en-

Bonifacio is dramatically set above chalk cliffs

closing the landward side of the old town, whose medieval houses seem almost to be toppling off the end of the island and into the sea. The upper town is a maze of narrow streets flanked by tall tenements, rising seamlessly out of the sheer cliffs.

Take a boat cruise to the nature reserve on the island of **Lavezzi** and you can swim or snorkel in the clear waters surrounded by enormous sculpted white rocks. Also worthwhile is the walk along the clifftops to the east of town. Other typical excursions from Bonifacio include a visit to the attractive hill towns around **Propriano** and **Porto Vecchio**.

Italy

Climate In the cruise ports of Italy, winters are fairly mild, and hot, dry summers are tempered by sea-breezes (more along the Tyrrhenian coastline than the Adriatic). Summers can be torrid in the south and on the islands.

Time Zone GMT+1 (+2 in summer).

Opening Times Shops are open 9am–12.30pm and 3.30/4–7.30/8pm. In areas serving tourists, hours are generally longer; for instance in Venice, many shops remain open on Sunday, while elsewhere almost everything is closed on that day. Shops often also close on Monday (sometimes in the morning only) and some shut on Saturday.

What to Buy With an unrivalled reputation for fashion, Italy is a mecca for the style-conscious, with a huge range of designer clothes and accessories that fill the pages of glossy magazines. Equally deep pockets are required for the better historic prints; ceramics, too, are usually expensive.

Money Matters Euro.

Festivals and Public Holidays 1 January, Good Friday, Easter Monday, 25 April, 1 May, 15 August, 1 November, 8, 25, 26 December. In addition to these national holidays, almost all cities have their own holidays to celebrate their patron saint.

Etiquette Visitors wearing unsuitable (skimpy) dress may be barred from entering churches. Smoking is banned from public places.

Tipping Italians don't always tip in restaurants. Most restaurants continue to impose an outdated cover and bread charge (*pane and coperto*), although it has been officially eliminated in most cities. Often, in addition, a 10 percent service charge is added to the bill. If service is not included, 12–15 percent is usual.

Hazards and Security Beware of bag snatchers from cars and avoid displaying valuables. Venice is one of Italy's safest cities.

Emergency Telephone Numbers Police 112; general emergency 113; fire 115; paramedics 118.

Gondola on the Grand Canal in Venice

ITALY

The western and eastern coasts of Italy were at one time dominated by the single ports of Genoa and Venice respectively. Both had powerful mercantile interests protected by forts outside Italy.

Today, cruise ships on the west coast offer access mainly to the glories of Florence, Siena and Rome, although Genoa and Naples are vibrant cities in their own right, and the ports on the stunning Amalfi coast attract smaller ships. From Naples, the natural firework display that is volcanic Stromboli is a highlight on the way to Sardinia, which combines sun-kissed beaches and a ruggedly beautiful interior with cosmopolitan chic. On the east coast, a visit to the extraordinary, labyrinthine city of Venice is alone worth a trip. Though the ports of Sicily, the Mediterranean's largest island, are unmistakeably Italian, their affinity with nearby North Africa is highly evident.

Genoa

Seen from the industrial port area where cruise ships dock, **Genoa** (Genova) crowds attractively over the hills. The city has a merchant history stretching back to the 5th century. Its golden age was the 14th century, when Genoese ports and colonies stretched as far as the Black Sea.

There are two neighbouring cruise terminals; the large two-level Stazzione Maritima at Ponte dei Mille and the 1930s' terminal at Ponte Andrea Doria. A new terminal and extra cruise-ship berth at the Ponte Parodi, close to Genoa's historic old town, should open in 2007.

Making friends with the pigeons by the port

The **Porto Antico** (Old Port), with its wonderfully restored waterfront, is a short walk away (turn right when you exit the docks and follow the main road). Highlights include the **Galata Museo del Mare** (Museum of the Sea; open Tues–Sun, Mar–Oct 10am–7.30pm, Nov–Feb 10am–6pm; admission fee). and the **Acquario** (acquarium; open Mon 10am–6pm, Tues–Fri 9.30am–7.30pm, Sat–Sun 9.30am–8.30pm; admission fee).

Inland from the harbour is the lively street market of the **Piazza Banchi**. A *trompe-l'oeil* church – the **Chiesa di San Pietro della Porta** – was built in the 16th century above the commercial buildings on the square. Also here is the 18th-century **Loggia dei Mercanti**, a massive, marble-floored hall that once housed the stock exchange.

Lion guarding San Lorenzo

Southwest of here is the Old Town, which is characterised by narrow, twisting and sometimes very steep streets and best explored on foot. Tucked away on Piazza della Santa Maria Magdalene is the **Chiesa Santa Maria Magdalene**, a church with a vastly opulent interior.

The hub of the city is **Piazza Ferrari**, a wide-open space with a fountain as its centrepiece. The chic shopping streets Via XX Settembre, Via Roma and Via XXV Aprile converge with Via Dante here. The **Palazzo Ducale** (open 9am–9pm, admission fee) borders the northwest side of the square; its interior has a large vaulted room and an airy columned courtyard.

On Piazza San Lorenzo, is the 13th-century black-and-white marble **Duomo** (cathedral; open Mon–Sat 9–11.30am, 3–6pm; admission fee), also known as San Lorenzo. With shallow Gothic arches and steps flanked by reclining lions, this is an outstanding Pisan-style building and campanile.

For designer shopping, try the stores in **Via Roma**. Small antiques and carpet shops and an Illy café nestle in **Via XXV Aprile**, which is popular with the expensively dressed set at lunch. Through the arch of the Galleria Garibaldi tunnel, **Via Garibaldi** is lined with 16th-century mansions and *palazzos* built with the wealth that came from the city's maritime power.

For a panoramic overview of Genoa, the port and the Mediterranean, a **cable car** runs from the Piazza dell'Annunziata up to the ancient fortifications.

Looking over Portofino harbour

Portofino

Meaning 'Port of Dolphins', **Portofino** has been a magnet for the beautiful people since the 19th century, and it's easy to see why: with clear, deep green waters, it's a gorgeous, tiny natural harbour, set below a steep, wooded bay. The port does not have a dock for liners, so a tender service ferries passengers to shore.

Portofino is seemingly more of a fishing and sailing harbour than a resort, but look and you'll find some fine 'extremely exclusive' hotels and private villas back in the forest-covered hills. From the colourfully painted houses clustered around the postage stamp-sized harbour, avoid the crowds by setting out on a paved cliff walk. Pass the yellow-painted church of San Giorgio to the lighthouse *(faro)* at the end of the government-protected promontory, Monte Portofino, for a superb view along the coast. The cliffs are clothed in a profusion of exotic vegetation, with occasional glimpses of private homes framed by cypresses, palm trees and cascades of bougainvillaea.

An inexpensive and frequent boat service runs between Portofino and the **Abbazia di San Fruttuoso** (open daily Mar–Apr and Oct 10am–4pm, May–Sept 10am–6pm; Dec–Feb 10am–6pm on holidays only; admission fee). The Abbazia (abbey) contains exhibits of exquisite amber, pottery from the 13th to the 15th century and historic masonry from the abbey, all with helpful annotations and almost all in Italian. The cloisters give lovely views of the bay.

Portovenere

A visit to **Portovenere** is a highlight of any Mediterranean  cruise. Perched at the end of a thin promontory, its tall, coloured buildings crowd against the steep slopes, with the cliffs of the Cinque Terre plunging into the aquamarine sea around – a magical setting best appreciated from the sea.

Cruise ships cannot dock in Portovenere, so those going ashore are tendered in. The waterfront has the usual collection of tourist shops, attractive pavement cafés and fish restaurants. The tourist office is set at the back of the small Piazza Bastreri to the right of the waterfront.

Most people head for the marble-and-granite-striped church of **San Pietro**, superbly situated at the end of the promontory. From the terrace, there are views towards the Cinque Terre. A staircase leads up to **Grotta Arpaia**, known as Byron's Grotto. This stretch of coast is linked to the English Romantic

Brightly coloured buildings in Portovenere

poets: Byron lived in a villa in nearby La Spezia. However, in 1822 his friend Shelley was drowned while attempting to sail from Livorno to Lerici, where he had a house.

Narrow backstreets and flights of steps lead steeply up to the Romanesque parish church of **San Lorenzo**. Directly above is the **Castle** (open daily Apr–Oct 10am–noon, 2– 6pm, Nov–Mar 2–5pm; admission fee); in medieval times Porto-venere was a fortified outpost of the Republic of Genoa, but the Genoese structure was largely dismantled in 1453, and the present castle is baroque. Via G. Capellini, with attractive old houses and quaint shops, leads back down to Piazza Bastreri.

Excursions from Portovenere

Full-day excursions usually go to Pisa *(see page 105)*, Florence *(see page 102)* or the Cinque Terre. Boats also serve **I**sola Palmaria, colonised by Benedictine monks in medieval times.

The quintessential Riviera: UNESCO-protected Corniglia

Cinque Terre ('Five Lands') is the collective name for the five villages of Monterosso al Mare, Vernazza, Corniglia, Manarola and Riomaggiore. Clinging like eagles' nests to the rocky coast just north of Portovenere – a stretch of

> The area around Genoa, the western side of Liguria, is called Ponente – a reference to where the sun sets. Eastern Liguria is known as the Levante – a reference to the rising sun.

land described by Byron as 'paradise on earth' – these villages, characterised by steep, narrow streets, colourful houses and tiny squares, form a UNESCO World Heritage site, with the surrounding area a designated National Park. Since access to them by car is virtually impossible, they have been spared mass tourism. This makes conditions even more ideal for the many hikers who come here for the well-marked routes and breathtaking views.

Livorno (Florence)

Founded in the 16th century by the Grand Dukes of Tuscany – the Medici family – **Livorno** has been a key Italian port ever since and is now Italy's third largest. Sadly many of the city's baroque and Renaissance villas were destroyed by World War II bombing, and the rebuilt city had become somewhat rundown by the 1990s. However, it is now showing signs of greater prosperity – helped by the increasing number of cruise ships calling here.

For most cruise visitors, however, Livorno is simply the gateway to Florence, Pisa *(see page 105)* and the Tuscan towns of Siena *(see page 107)* and Lucca *(see page 108)* and their surrounding countryside. All places are accessible on organised tours or can be visited independently (either by train – best value – or by taxi, which may work out less expensive than an organised tour if you travel in a group of two or more).

Florence

Florence (Firenze), approximately 1½–2 hours by train from Livorno, was the cradle of the Renaissance, the momentous 'rebirth' of Classical ideals that saw European art and architecture, philosophy and politics make a decisive break with the medieval past. Despite floods, war and bombing, the city has managed to preserve much of its Renaissance heritage – frescoed churches and palaces, public buildings, sculptures and many renowned works of art can all be admired here. It is relatively small city – mostly pedestrianised – so it's easily navigable on foot; the Arno River, which cuts the city in two from east to west, is useful for keeping one's bearings.

The rooftops of Florence from the Duomo's cupola

The cavernous 13th-century Dominican church of Santa Maria Novella, with a graceful white-and-green marble facade added by Leon Battista Alberti in 1470, is a good place to start a tour. Among its treasures, in the left aisle, third bay, is one of the city's greatest paintings, the *Masaccio Trinity*, famed for its early handling of perspective and depth.

Head east of here towards San Lorenzo, designed by Brunelleschi before he created the Duomo's cupola. The church is renowned for its exquisite Medici chapels, monuments to this great family dynasty.

Southeast of here, on **Piazza del Duomo**, the assembled buildings represent a textbook on the landmarks of the Renaissance. The little **Battistero** (Baptistery), situated to the west of the cathedral, is adorned with truly magnificent doors of sculpted bronze. The competition to design these doors pitted artist against artist, and in the competitive atmos-

Bridges straddle the Arno

phere of the early 15th-century, new artistic ideas were born that saw the stylised religious art of the Middle Ages left behind in favour of greater realism.

In architecture, new heights were achieved – quite literally, as the dome of the huge cathedral illustrates. Nobody had dared build such a dome since Roman times, and Brunelleschi spent years studying Rome's 1st-century AD Pantheon dome in order to prepare for this great feat. Alongside, the delicately patterned campanile, clad in marble of green, pink and white, is known as Giotto's bell tower, after the great 14th-century artist who designed it in 1334.

From here, make for the **Piazza della Signoria**, home to an astonishing assemblage of outdoor statuary, monumental fountains and palatial buildings. This square has witnessed many great events in Florentine history, including the burning at the stake of the revolutionary firebrand preacher Savonarola, in 1498. He died in the battle for power that republican-minded citizens waged against the powerful Medici princes, who ruled this city for almost 500 years. Note the copy (the original is in the Accademia gallery) of Michelangelo's huge statue of **David**.

The Uffizi's *Birth of Venus* by Botticelli

Directly south, close to the banks of the Arno, is the world-renowned **Galleria degli Uffizi** (Uffizi Gallery; open Tues–Sun 8.15am– 6.30pm; admission fee), designed by the architect Vasari to house the Medici administration (Uffizi simply means 'offices'). The building is now a showcase of Italian and other European painting, with highlights including Botticelli's *Birth of Venus* and *Allegory of Spring*, Michelangelo's *Doni Tondo* and works by Leonardo, Raphael, Titian and Giotto.

Just west of here is the **Ponte Vecchio**. This 'Old Bridge', dating from 1345, has covered shops on both sides of its central carriageway, and these are occupied by the city's goldsmiths, perpetuating a centuries-old tradition.

East of the Uffizi is the church of **Santa Croce**, known as the Florentine Pantheon because so many renowned Florentines are buried here. As you tour the aisles, look out for the tombs of Michelangelo, Machiavelli and even Galileo (he was buried here in 1737, though for years the Church refused him Christian burial because of his 'heresy' in stating that the earth orbits the sun). At the eastern end of the church, gorgeously coloured and minutely detailed frescoes showing scenes from the *Life of Christ* are the work of Giotto, the 14th-century artist whom many consider to be the father of Renaissance art. He not only learned the art of fresco painting (long forgotten in the West) from itinerant Greek artists, he also achieved new heights of artistic expression and realism in his work, which was widely copied and admired.

If time allows, make for Piazzale Michelangelo, an excellent place to find your bearings. This large square, decorated with reproductions of Michelangelo masterpieces, looks out over the whole city. Down below is the Arno, while over to the left is the magnificent dome of the Duomo, soaring over the terracotta rooftops.

Pisa

In its heyday from the 11th to the 13th century, **Pisa** (20 minutes from Livorno by train) was at the centre of a maritime empire down the Tyrrhenian coast and in Corsica, Sardinia, Sicily, Syria, Palestine and Egypt. Its prestige called for a legacy, and the funds were provided for a marble complex of religious edifices (Duomo, Campanile – the Leaning Tower – and Baptistery), known as the **Campo dei Miracoli** (Field of Miracles). The **Duomo** (open daily Mar 9am–6pm, Apr–Sept 8am–8pm, Oct–Feb 9am–5pm; admission fee) was begun in 1063 during the Golden Age, to honour Pisa's victory over the Saracens in Sicily. Architect Buscheto didn't hesitate to write in Latin (in the far left arch): 'This marble church has no equal.'

Thanks to its unstable subsoil, the **Campanile** (Leaning Tower; open daily Apr–Sept 8am–8pm; Mar, Oct

Pisa's Leaning Tower

9am–6pm; all other months 9am–5pm; admission fee; advanced reservation only, tel: 050 560547; <www.duomo. pisa.it>) has always tilted. Begun in 1173, it started to lean when only three of its eight storeys had been completed. The overhang increased over time and by the late 20th century it was 4.5m (15ft) out of alignment. Fearing an imminent collapse, the authorities closed the tower in 1990, while engineers sought a remedy. It was finally decided that soil should be extracted from the foundations on the opposite side to the lean and by early 2001 the top of the tower had been brought

Florentine Writers

Dante Alighieri (1265–1321), member of a Guelph family, was exiled by a faction of his party for the last 19 years of his life. His immortal poetic work, *The Divine Comedy*, describing a journey through Hell and Purgatory to arrive at last in Paradise, is one of the great landmarks of world literature. In it he juxtaposes divinely ordained political and social order with the ugly reality of the corrupt society around him. Dante was the first to write his masterpiece not in the usual scholarly Latin, but in his everyday language, thus establishing the Tuscan vernacular as 'pure Italian' spoken today and used as the language of literature.

Petrarch (Francesco Petrarca, 1304–74), born in Arezzo, was the son of a Florentine lawyer. Poet, scholar and a lifelong friend of Boccaccio, he was regarded as one of the most learned men of his time, and was instrumental in the rediscovery of Classical literature that laid the basis for the flowering of Renaissance lyric poetry. He is best known for poems to 'Laura', in which he expresses an idealised, unrequited love.

Giovanni Boccaccio (1313–75) was a Classical scholar and university lecturer, specialising in the works of Dante. Survivor of the Black Death, he used his experiences as the basis for his prose tales, *The Decameron*. Written in an Italian still easily understood, the work is unrivalled for its gentle eroticism, humour and vivid characterisation.

back 45cm (18in) – a 10 percent reduction in inclination. The tower has reopened to the public, with up to 30 people at a time allowed up the 293 steps of the narrow spiral staircase (tours every 40 minutes).

Siena

Around 34km (21 miles) south of Florence, **Siena** is still a medieval hilltop city. Its walls enclose a maze of narrow, winding streets that have survived virtually unchanged since the 16th century and earlier. The city itself is a wonderful marriage of brick and stone, all weathered reds and warm

Inside the striped Duomo, Siena

pinks (hence the term 'burnt sienna'). Imposing Gothic architecture prevails within the city walls, from the main square's early 14th-century Palazzo Pubblico, with its graceful and slender 97m (320ft) tower, the Torre del Mangia, to the grand zebra-striped cathedral and many fine palazzi.

The heart of the city is the huge, sloping, fan-shaped **Piazza del Campo** (commonly known as Il Campo), where the Palio horse race takes place twice each summer, with tickets virtually impossible to obtain. Almost all of historic Siena is closed to traffic. Wander freely through the picturesque, winding and hilly streets to the great Gothic **Duomo**. Perched atop Siena's highest point and begun in 1196, it's striking black-and-white striped exterior is visible from afar.

Lucca

Dante, Petrarch and Boccaccio all wrote in the Tuscan dialect, and in the 16th century it became the official national language, a fact of which Tuscans are justifiably proud.

The 'sights' of **Lucca** take scarcely a day, but the seductive tranquillity within its perfectly preserved ramparts is irresistible. Things were not always so peaceful here. In the stormy 15th and 16th centuries, Lucca's silk merchants preserved the peace by paying enemy armies to bypass the town. It has been particularly rich in musicians, notably Boccherini and Puccini, and hosts music festivals in summer.

Begin with a stroll on the tree-shaded pathway atop the brick 16th–17th century ramparts, along the Passeggiata delle Mura, for a good overall view of the town's traffic-free *centro storico* contained within the walls. Key sights include the **Duomo San Martino** (open Sun–Fri 9.30am–5.45pm, Sat 9.30am–6.45pm; free), begun in 1060 and with a Pisan-style facade, and, northwest of the cathedral, **San Michele in Foro**, on the site of the Roman Forum. To capture something of the town's medieval character, explore the Via Guinigi, with smart 14th-century palaces, and the towered houses of Via Fillungo, leading to the Roman amphitheatre, now the Piazza del Mercato.

Elba

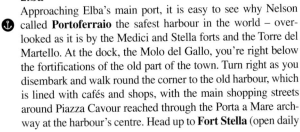

Approaching Elba's main port, it is easy to see why Nelson called **Portoferraio** the safest harbour in the world – overlooked as it is by the Medici and Stella forts and the Torre del Martello. At the dock, the Molo del Gallo, you're right below the fortifications of the old part of the town. Turn right as you disembark and walk round the corner to the old harbour, which is lined with cafés and shops, with the main shopping streets around Piazza Cavour reached through the Porta a Mare archway at the harbour's centre. Head up to **Fort Stella** (open daily

9am–8pm; free) or simply go straight uphill from the dock to reach the Medici fort. At the far side of Fort Stella from the harbour is the residence of Elba's best-known resident, Napoleon. Most of the charm of his **Villa dei Mulini** (open Mar–Oct Mon–Sat 9am–7pm, Sun 9am–1pm; admission fee) lies in the period furnishings and Italianate gardens.

If you have a full day you can reach pretty much anywhere on Elba by taxi. Buses depart every hour from near the port (turn left) in the new part of town to Napoleon's summer residence, **San Martino** (open Mar–Oct Mon–Sat 9am–7pm, Sun 9am–1pm; admission fee), which is only 6km (4 miles) away. The compact villa has exquisite views down to Portoferraio.

The spectacular drive westward from Portoferraio to **Marciana Marina** passes a number of popular beaches, including Le Ghiaie, noted for its multicoloured pebbles, and La Biodola, considered the chicest beach on Elba.

Portoferraio's Fort Stella, on Elba

Civitavecchia (Rome)

⚓ **Civitavecchia** was commissioned as a port in 106BC by the Emperor Trajan, because it was in the ideal geographical position to serve the city of Rome. It continues to do so today and is one of Italy's best-equipped ports. Civitavecchia is the start or finish point of many cruises, but those ships passing through will normally spend a full day here to allow passengers to visit Rome, some 80km (50 miles) to the southeast.

Rome

Organised cruise-line excursions to **Rome** (Roma), a highlight of any Mediterranean cruise, are always available, but it's quite easy to travel independently by train, which takes just 50–75 minutes. For the Vatican, get off at San Pietro station if possible, otherwise stay on until Termini, the main terminus for Rome. Make sure to validate your return ticket

St Peter's Square

by punching it in one of the machines on the platform.

A walk in the Eternal City is a stroll through the history of Western civilisation. Ancient ruins, magnificent churches and works of Renaissance art combine with the energy and colour of modern Italy to make this one of the world's most fascinating cities. Its incredible history has seen it become the epicentre of one of the largest and most powerful empires the world has ever

The Spanish Steps

seen; the home of the Catholic Church and, as such, a place of pilgrimage for millions; one of the major centres of the world-changing 15th-century Renaissance; and the capital of the Italian nation state. You cannot properly explore Rome in a single day, but even a short visit is immensely rewarding.

Within easy walking distance of Termini station are both the **Museo Nazionale Romano** (four sites; admission fee), which holds many of Rome's important antiquities; and the sumptuous 17th-century Palazzo Barberini, which houses the **Galleria Nazionale de Arte Antica** (open Tues–Sun 9am–7pm; admission fee), displaying some wonderful paintings by Lippi, El Greco and Caravaggio, among others. Visiting them, then having a leisurely lunch or a drink at any one of the outdoor cafés and restaurants still leaves time to return to the ship.

By the foot of the **Scalla di Spagna** (Spanish Steps; Spagna metro station) stands the pink house where John Keats, the English romantic poet, died. For shoppers, Dior, Gucci and Moschino cluster among the retail temples nearby. The steps themselves are a magnetic draw for travellers, musicians and street merchants peddling T-shirts, leatherwear and jewellery. Make the climb to the top and you'll be rewarded by a view across the Roman roofline to the Vatican and the seven hills of the city. At the top are upmarket art galleries.

The **Fontana di Trevi** (Trevi Fountain), within walking distance of the Spanish Steps, is the most popular coin collector in Europe. The story goes that if you want to return to Rome, you should stand with your back to the fountain, and toss a coin over your shoulder and into the water. Another legend has it that the offering will assure your return to the sea, a safe bet for cruisers. The fountain was built as the front of the church of **Santi Vincenzo e Anastasio** by sculptor Nicola Salvi between 1732 and 1762.

The Colosseum

The ruins of the Stadium of Domitian, the scene of Roman chariot races, lie beneath the **Piazza Navona**; popes in medieval times flooded the square to stage sea battles. Now free from flooding, combat and traffic, the splendid piazza is a great place for lunch or a drink. Eat a thin, crisp Roman pizza, or lunch at one of the fine restaurants. Marvel at Bernini's **Fontana dei Fiumi** (Four Rivers Fountain) and watch people having fun by the water. In the evening, the piazza serves as an open-air gallery for Roman artists.

One of the great remains of the ancient world is the imposing **Colosseo** (Colosseum; open daily, 9am–3/4/4.30/5/7pm depending on time of year; admission fee). Formerly clad in marble, at its height it could seat 50,000 for the 'bread and circuses' spectacles. It opened in AD80 with a bloody combat between gladiators and wild beasts lasting for weeks, and it is believed that the arena could be flooded for sea battles.

The Vatican

In AD324, Emperor Constantine declared Christianity to be the official religion of the Roman Empire, and the first Christian churches were built in the city. But with the empire in decline, Constantine moved the imperial seat to Constantinople – formerly Byzantium and now Istanbul, although the papacy remained in Rome. The **Citta del Vaticano** (Vatican City) is a self-contained sovereign state, and with only 400 passport-holders, is one of the world's tiniest nations. For many, this is Rome's most important site. The crowds are usually large, so a visit here can take up much of the day.

Bernini's spectacularly Doric-colonnaded **Piazza San Pietro** (St Peter's Square) is overlooked by the statues of 140 saints. This immense space forms the entrance to the **Basilica**

The Seven Hills

Italy's capital is built on seven hills – Aventine, Capitoline, Celio, Esquiline, Palatine, Quirinale and Viminale – around the River Tiber 35km (22 miles) from the sea. The city, the Comune di Roma, has a population of nearly three million and occupies 1,507 sq km (582 sq miles) including the independent city state of the Vatican, which takes up less than half a square kilometre. On the same latitiude as New York, Rome has a mild climate, but summers can be hot and the best time to visit is in spring or early autumn.

di San Pietro (St Peter's Basilica; open daily Oct–Mar 9am–5.15pm, Apr–Sept till 6.15pm; admission fee), built at the order of Emperor Constantine in AD324. St Peter is believed to have been crucified at the Circus of Nero, to the left of the site.

Some of the greatest art of the Christian world is in the **Musei e Gallerie del Vaticano** (open summer Mon–Fri 8.45am–3.45pm, Sat and last Sun of month 8.45am–1.45pm; winter Mon–Sat and last Sun 8.45am–1.45pm; admission fee). The vast collections can hardly be sampled in a day, so aim for a few highlights, such as the frescoes by Botticelli, Pinturiccino and Ghilrandaio in the **Cappella Sistina** (Sistine Chapel) and the spectacular ceiling by Michaelangelo.

Naples

The vast Bay of Naples is dominated by the hazy, cone-shaped mass of Mt Vesuvius, slumbering behind the urban

The Bay of Naples, with Mt Vesuvius in the background

sprawl of the city. **Naples** (Napoli), along with pretty Sorrento, the glamorous island of Capri, and Amalfi, on the Gulf of Salerno to the south, are the major ports of call for Pompeii, Herculaneum, Mt Vesuvius and the gorgeous, romantic Amalfi Coast – the usual destinations of ship excursions.

Naples' Castel Nuovo

Even by Italian standards, Naples seems to be a city in a state of permanent chaos, with all of its 1.5 million-plus inhabitants apparently on the roads at the same time. It has the country's second-busiest port, which is the hub of the city, with the most interesting sights within a short radius. A €500m-project is underway to transform parts of the city, including the port area. Refurbishment of the cruise terminal is completing in 2005, and other improvements will include the creation of a pedestrianised promenade and a yacht marina.

Currently, though, Naples's appearance on so many cruise itineraries is due to its location rather than its own attractions. Not only are the major archaeological sites of Pompeii and Herculaneum just a few kilometres away, the city is also the gateway to the Amalfi Coast. Naples is rarely used as a home port. The infrastructure is there but cruise lines prefer to use it as a port of call (always a full-day stay) to enable passengers to choose from a variety of shore excursions.

Cruising into the Bay of Naples is a memorable experience: the impressive entrance into the port is overlooked by an imposing medieval castle, Sant' Elmo, high on Vemero Hill, and another, the 13th-century Castel Nuovo, stands right where

Typical old Neapolitan street, festooned with washing

the ships dock, either side of a large terminal building, the Stazione Maritima.

Once outside the terminal, you are in the heart of Naples. Although the main city appears to extend to the right, the most interesting part is the old quarter, straight ahead past Castel Nuovo and over the Piazza Municipio, or to the left towards the Piazza Plebiscito. Also immediately to the left is Molo Beverello – the dock and ticket station for the ferry and hydrofoil services to the resort of Sorrento and the isle of Capri.

One of the pleasures of Naples is just wandering the narrow old streets. The noise of the ubiquitous scooters and car horns means it probably won't be quiet, and you should be very careful about your valuables, but this is the best way to soak up the ambience. Although there are short city tours on offer, they devote most of the time to scenic drives outside Naples. The only real way to see what the city has to offer is on foot. Within a 15-minute walk from the terminal there are three of the city's best-known sights: the **Castel Nuovo**, with an extraordinary Renaissance arch; the **Palazzo Reale** (open Tues–Sat 9am–7pm; admission fee), with a monumental marble staircase; and the ornate, 18th-century **Teatro San Carlo**, the largest opera house in Italy.

A longer walk (or short taxi ride) across the Piazza Municipio and up Via Toledo brings you to a fourth place of interest – the **Museo Archeològico Nazionale** (open Mon, Wed–Sun 9am–7pm; admission fee), one of the world's finest archaeological collections, with a huge treasure of finds from Pompeii and Herculaneum *(see page 118)*.

Amalfi

In early medieval times, **Amalfi** was a significant maritime power, Italy's main trading port, and home to some 80,000 people. Now a small, busy town that prospers through the tourist industry, Amalfi gives its name to the stretch of craggy Italian coast between Sorrento and Salerno. Even the smaller cruise ships have to anchor off and tender passengers ashore. Ships usually stay a full day, although sometimes only a half-day stay is scheduled.

Cruising into the sheltered harbour of Amalfi is one of the most attractive approaches in Mediterranean cruising. With its red-tiled roofs contrasting with the Spanish-style whitewashed houses, the town nestles at the foot of a steeply sloped wooded gorge. Tenders bring you right into the heart of town and, although there is no terminal, the quayside (at Piazza Flavio Gioia) is just across the road from a taxi rank, tourist information centre, telephones, banks and currency exchange bureaux and only 100m/yds from the main square, Piazza Duomo.

The switchback Amalfi Coast

Most of the shops are aimed at tourists, which means that they are open all day but that they are not the best places for buying quality goods. There are some interesting handicrafts, though, and you can't avoid bottles of Limoncello, the locally made lemon-based liqueur.

Pompeii and Herculaneum

In the 1st century AD, **Pompeii** was a prosperous port at the mouth of the Sarno River. What happened to its 20,000 citizens in August AD79 was not as sudden as a bomb blast, but just as devastating. There had been warnings, and a bad earthquake 17 years earlier, although Vesuvius was green to its crest with vineyards and never considered threatening. Tremors shook the earth for several days in late August. Then around noon on 24 August a mushroom cloud shot up from the mountain and obscured the sun. A torrent of ashes, cinders and pumice pebbles fell on to the surrounding settlements. The earth shuddered repeatedly and tidal waves rolled in from the sea. Terrified people fled, on foot and by boat. The roofs of buildings collapsed under the weight of volcanic debris. For three days it continued. When the sky cleared on 27 August, Pompeii was buried under 7m (23ft) of ash, which solidified with rain and time, preserving everything it encased. Pompeii remained hidden until 1594, when workmen tunnelling for an aqueduct unearthed walls and tablets. Serious excavations were begun in 1748.

While Pompeii was crushed under falling volcanic debris and red-hot cinders, the ancient town of **Herculaneum** was filled from the bottom up by ash and pumice carried on a torrent of superheated gas. The city was covered to an average depth of 20m (65ft). Until 1980 only a few bodies had been found here, and it was believed that Herculaneum's estimated 5,000 inhabitants had managed to escape. In 1980 came the discovery of hundreds of skeletons of men, women and children who had taken shelter in vaults at the marina. These skeletons provided a rare opportunity to study the size and health of typical Romans, for they cremated their dead, and cemeteries contain only urns with ashes.

Amalfi is a compact town so a walking tour is easy to do on your own. The main attraction – apart from its many cafés, seafood restaurants, shops and a small beach – is the cathedral, the **Duomo di Sant' Andrea**, with attractive cloisters and crypt, in Piazza Duomo. This dates from the 9th century but has been rebuilt and restored many times. A short walk further inland from the square you'll find a paper museum (in a former paper mill) and the Limoncello factory. Walk east along the waterfront for 10 minutes from the quayside to reach a former convent, now a hotel (Luna Convento) with a separate restaurant built into a fort overlooking the sea. Another 5–10 minutes' walk brings you to the smaller, less touristy town of **Atrani**.

Pompeiian finds illustrate the Romans' lifestyle

Other Excursions from Naples and Amalfi

The pretty island of **Capri**, celebrated in song as the Island of Dreams and famed for its abundant floral displays in the warm months; **Sorrento** (the *grande dame* of Neapolitan resorts); and the archaeological sites of **Pompeii** and **Herculaneum** *(see box opposite)* are usually offered as full-day excursions from Naples and Amalfi; the **Emerald Grotto** is usually available as a short boat trip.

Gondolas moored along the Grand Canal

Venice

An inspiration for writers and artists down the centuries, **Venice** (Venezia) continues to cast a spell over its many visitors. It's hard to imagine another city more richly deserving of its status as a World Heritage site. It is just about the perfect cruise call because everything is so easily accessible; cars are banned, making it a pleasure to explore the maze of narrow cobbled streets and nearly 500 historic bridges at its heart.

Bustling Piazza di San Marco (St Mark's Square) and the ancient Basilica di San Marco, the lavish Palazzo Ducale (Doge's Palace), the imposing Campanile, the shop-lined Rialto Bridge across the Grand Canal – these are the famous icons, but the beauty of Venice is also in the detail, in the exposure to daily life in surroundings seemingly unchanged by the passage of time.

Venice is never quiet, but there are certainly fewer people around in the spring, autumn and winter than in summer. This makes for easier sightseeing and shopping but there can also be occasional flooding, with duck-boards out in St Mark's Square.

Many lines use Venice as a home port for one or more of their ships; for other lines, it is a port of call within a cruise. The main docking area is beyond St Mark's Square, so your ship will sail past it on its way into port. If you are on one of the larger mega-ships, make sure you are on an upper deck, as this affords a spectacular view across the centre of the city and the outlying lagoon islands.

Some lines offer a canal shuttle to Piazza San Marco from the main docks. Alternatively, the *vaporetto* (water bus) station is right by the terminals. The fastest route is No. 34. If you plan to make more than four *vaporetto* trips during your stay, it pays to buy a day ticket *(gionaliero)*. While frequent and inexpensive, the *vaporettos* are a slow way to get around because of their many stops. Water-taxis are faster but much more expensive while, for the longer journeys across the Grand Canal, gondola ferries *(traghettos)* are the best option.

Some ships dock at San Basilio, a little way away from the main cruise terminals but on *vaporetto* routes, and at Riva Sette Martiri, from where you can walk to St Mark's via a series of nine bridges and past the famous Hotel Danieli. This takes 10–15 minutes.

Venetian mask

Piazza di San Marco

Piazza di San Marco (St Mark's Square), dubbed by Napoleon 'the finest drawing room in Europe', is the heart and soul of Venice and the best place to start your tour. The lavish basilica that dominates it, the **Basilica di San**

Golden Screen

Behind the altar in the Basilica di San Marco is the Pala d'Oro (Golden Screen), an altar screen featuring dozens of scenes from the Bible. Its exquisitely wrought golden frame holds the Venetian equivalent of the Crown Jewels: 1,300 pearls, 400 garnets, 300 sapphires, 300 emeralds, 90 amethysts, 75 balas-rubies, 15 rubies, 4 topazes and 2 cameos.

Marco (open Apr–Sept Mon–Sat 9.30am–5.30pm, Sun 2–5.30pm, Oct–Mar Mon–Sat 10am–4.30pm, Sun 2–4.30pm; free), was built in 832 (although since reconstructed several times) to house the relics of St Mark. The Evangelist's relics were stolen from their grave in Alexandria by a group of Venetian merchants. The theft was seen as an act of Christian piety, rescuing holy relics from a land ruled by Muslim infidels. The whole story is told in the glittering mosaics in the basilica's atrium.

Inside the church, every surface is decorated with marble and mosaics, with Christ in Majesty on the ceiling of the central dome. As well as St Mark's body, most of the materials used to build the church were also stolen or looted as spoils of war. Among the looted treasures were the **Four Horses of San Marco**, ancient Greek or Roman statues (no-one is quite sure which) cast in gilded bronze around AD200. These were stolen from the Hippodrome (racecourse) in Constantinople (now Istanbul) and placed on a balcony above the Basilica's main portal (those visible from the square are copies; the originals are inside the basilica's **Museo Marciano**). Plundered goldwork and jewel-encrusted Byzantine icons can be seen in the **Treasury**, which is full of fascinating relics from the earliest days of Christianity.

For the most breathtaking views of the Piazza and the city, take a lift to ascend the 100m (335ft) of Venice's tallest building, the **Campanile di San Marco** (St Mark's Bell tower; open daily Mar–Jun 9am–7pm, Jul–Sept 9am–9pm, Oct–Feb 9.30am–4pm; admission fee), which over the years has served as a lighthouse, gun turret and belfry. Within a minute, the exotic domes of the basilica, the splendid wedge-shaped tip of Dorsoduro (marking the start of the Grand Canal) and the island church of San Giorgio Maggiore all lie beneath your feet, while all around are the terracotta-coloured tiles of the ancient city roofscape. According to local lore, Galileo brought the doge up here to show off his new telescope. Intriguingly, not a single canal can be seen from the Campanile.

Gondolier on a break

Alongside the basilica is the **Palazzo Ducale** (Doge's Palace; open daily Mar–Oct 9am–5.30pm, Nov–Feb 9am–5pm; admission fee), the seat of Venetian government from the 9th to the 18th century. Magnificent frescoes by leading Venetian artists such as Veronese and Tintoretto decorate huge council chambers, where the doges once met their councillors.

From these stately rooms, it was just a short step to the city's notorious prisons, linked to the palace by the beautiful **Ponte dei Sospiri** (Bridge of Sighs) – nothing to do with languishing lovers, but named after the desperate sighs of those condemned to languish in the jail. Venetian-born Casanova was imprisoned for scandalous conduct, but the amorous adventurer daringly escaped from the jail by climbing through a hole in the lead-covered roof.

If you fancy a coffee while near St Mark's, why not visit Venetian institutions **Caffè Florian** and **Caffè Quadri**, the most prestigious cafés in the city. Be warned: it won't come cheap.

Along the Grand Canal

Moving away from the square, take a *vaporetto* along the Grand Canal and admire one historic building after another. Opposite the Piazzetta di San Marco is the magnificent baroque church of

---

Gondolas and Gondoliers

Nothing is more quintessentially Venetian than the gondola, although nowadays they are more a tourist attraction than a means of transport. Gondolas have existed since the 11th century, and in the 18th century around 14,000 plied Venice's canals; today, the city has fewer than 500. All gondolas are made to the same specifications, built by hand from around 280 separate pieces of wood. Curiously, they are asymmetrical (the left side is wider than the right) in order to accommodate the gondolier as he rows and steers. Gondolas are painted black in deference to the sumptuary laws of 1562 that attempted to curb the extravagances of Venetian society. They also retain a rather curious metallic pronged prow (or *ferro*). Several explanations have been offered for the symbolism and shape of the *ferro*: some think that the blades represent the six districts of Venice; others maintain that the shape suggests the Grand Canal or even the doge's cap. Many gondoliers still wear the traditional outfit of straw boater, striped T-shirt and white sailor's top. These days, if you want to be serenaded, that will cost extra.

Santa Maria della Salute (open daily 9am–noon and 3–6pm; free), known among the Venetians as 'la Salute'. It was built as an offering of thanks to the Virgin Mary for the end of a catastrophic plague in 1630 – the plague wiped out over a third of the lagoon's inhabitants. Head west towards the **Palazzo Venier dei Leoni**, which now houses the **Collezione Peggy Guggenheim** (open Wed–Mon 10am–6pm; admission fee), the bequest of American expatriate and heiress Peggy Guggenheim, and generally regarded as one of the best and most comprehensive collections of modern art

Towards Santa Maria della Salute

in Europe; while next to the nearby Accademia Bridge is the **Galleria dell'Accademia** (open Mon 8.15am–2pm, Tues–Sun 8am–7.15pm; admission fee), the most pre-eminent collection of Venetian art in existence and the most-visited spot in the city after Piazza San Marco and the Palazzo Ducale.

Lovers of Venetian art may also wish to head north to the church of **Madonna dell'Orto** (open Mon–Sat 10am–5pm, Sun 1–6pm; admission fee), a masterpiece of Venetian Gothic (take *vaporetto* No. 52 from Santa Lucia station). It is best known nowadays for its connections with the Renaissance painter Tintoretto – this was his parish church, and he is buried with his family to the right of the choir, near the high altar. The walls are decorated with his paintings.

Murano and Burano

If you want to see the islands of **Murano** or **Burano**, allow 30–45 minutes each way from St Mark's. If you have a full day, it's possible to see the main sights around St Mark's and either Murano or Burano as well, but allow ample time to return to your ship. It may be best to do your own tour around St Mark's and then book the ship's half-day excursion to Murano or Burano.

Murano is renowned worldwide as a historic glass-making centre. Although glass was manufactured in Venice as far back as the 10th century, the open furnaces presented such a fire hazard that around 1292 the Republic ordered the factories to be transferred to Murano. Grouped here, the glass blowers kept the secrets of their trade for centuries; the manufacture of mirrors, for instance, was for a long time exclusive to Venice.

Burano once produced the world's finest lace, and its delicate *punto in aria* pattern was the most sought after in

Burano's buildings are a rainbow of fabulous colours

Europe. Nowadays, the lace you see in local shops is largely imported from Asia, and real Burano lace is created by only a handful of women trained at the island's **Scuola del Merletto** (School of Lacemaking), on Piazza Galuppi.

Contemporary Murano glass

Verona

Shakespeare's 'Fair **Verona**' of *Romeo and Juliet* fame, with a Roman arena, splendid bridges and lovely churches, can be visited independently of excursions offered by cruise lines. There are trains around every hour from Venice's Santa Lucia station, and the journey time is around 1½ hours.

Once a thriving Roman settlement, Verona is now one of Italy's most prosperous, elegant cities. **Piazza Brà** is where the Veronese gather to talk, shop and drink in the shadow of the glorious 1st-century **Arena Romana** (Roman Arena; Tues–Sun 9am–6.30pm, Mon 1.45– 7.30pm; 8am–3.30pm in opera season, July–Aug; admission fee). On the north side of Piazza Brà, the Liston, lined with cafés and restaurants, leads to the boutiques, galleries and antiques shops of the chic Via Mazzini. Turn right at the end down Via Cappello for the 13th-century *palazzo* that the tourist authorities will have you believe was Juliet's House (Casa di Giulietta Cappelletti), complete with balcony.

Located in what is now Piazza delle Erbe, off Via Mazzini, is the **Foro Romano** (Roman Forum). This large open space has a quirky beauty due to the variety of *palazzi* and towers that line its sides. Among the most impressive is the baroque **Palazzo Maffei**, next to the **Torre del Gardello**, the tallest Gothic structure in the square.

Sardinia

As D.H. Lawrence did in the 20th century, contemporary travellers who are familiar with Italy find striking differences between the island of **Sardinia** and the mainland, but they will also discover many similarities. The beautiful beaches are some of the cleanest in the Mediterranean, while the expansive interior has opportunities for hiking, rock climbing and caving.

Cagliari, the Sardinian capital and chief port, has one of the best harbours in the Mediterranean. It rose to prominence as a Phoenician colony and Roman *castrum* (camp), becoming an important port on the east–west trading route. Cultural domination by successive waves of Pisans, Moors, Aragonese and Spanish has lent the city a faded cosmopolitan air and poignant aspirations to grandeur. Today, however, this is a quintessentially Mediterranean city.

Island fun on Sardinia

Cagliari

⚓ **Cagliari** is a busy ferry port with connections to Tunisia, Sicily, Naples, Livorno and Genoa. More recently, the city has successfully sought cruise ships as the best means of boosting tourism. Cagliari tends to be more favoured by Scandinavian, British and German cruise lines than the Italian-style cruise ships. Cruise ships moor by various jetties, with a free shuttle service dropping passengers off in the

Marina quarter in Cagliari

Stazione Marittima on the waterfront. The harbour is best seen during the evening promenade, the traditional parade of Italian one-upmanship known as the *passeggiata*. Parallel to the harbour is Via Roma, whose dignified arcades shelter traditional cafés and elegant boutiques.

Rather than embark on the usual excursion to see the archaeological site of Nora, some prefer to explore Cagliari independently, soaking up its distinctive Mediterranean atmosphere and indulging in people-watching, café-crawling and window-shopping for ceramics. This is also the best place on the island for a fish lunch, a fact that is even more significant given that Sardinia is better known for roast meats than seafood. The lazy way of seeing the old town of Cagliari is to hop aboard one of the tourist 'trains' which depart from Piazza Carmine in the Stampace quarter. There are several of these trains a day, except on Mondays during the off-season.

With a steep hill overlooking the port, Cagliari has an un-deniable down-at-heel charm. Stacked against the hillside is

Fabulous fresh fish, Sardinia

a higgledy-piggledy cluster of terracotta and ochre façades, many heavily ornamented with traditional arabesque designs. The principal sights include the ruins of a Roman amphitheatre and a Roman grid-style street pattern, framed by the bold medieval bastions that loom above the city.

Pastel-painted cottages and delicate wrought-iron balconies make the **San Domenico** district the best place to build up an appetite for lunch. From Piazza De Gasperi, on the eastern side of the port, take Via Gramsci northwards; this leads directly to the San Domenico district, close to the Romanesque cathedral.

The energetic can climb up to the Pisan-built **Citadella**, which has sweeping views over the old town, and retains its imposing 11th-century defensive walls. Others can get a taxi, or the summer tourist train, from the port and should ask for Citadella or the scenic Terrazzo Umberto.

If scenery is your main concern, the Bastion San Remy, with its palm, pine and oak trees, presents an imposing limestone and granite façade from where you'll have a spectacular view over the old districts of Cagliari, the pine woods, a beautiful lagoon and the surrounding mountains.

Only if you are desperate for a sandy beach is it worth stirring from Cagliari itself. If you feel so inclined, then, armed with a picnic, ask any taxi driver to take you to the lido at **Poetto**, set at the beginning of a huge sandy bay, 4km (2 miles) west of Cagliari, and agree a time for a return pick-up.

Sicily

If your ship calls at any of the Sicilian ports, you will immediately be aware of the historical winds of change that have swept over this central part of the Mediterranean. While Sicily could not be more Italian, it shows its affinity with North Africa, not so far across the water. Many visitors to Sicily head directly for the slopes of Mt Etna or to Taormina, about 40km (25 miles) down the coast. Taormina can also be reached by train or bus. Trips to Etna are best booked through a cruise company.

Palermo

Palermo's architecture, and Sicily's history, reflect the passing colonisation of the great Mediterranean empires – Carthage, Greece and Rome all made their mark here, as did the marauding Goths and Vandals, until the relative stability

Sailing in the waters around Sicily

Frescoes in Palermo

of joint Norman and Arab rule from 1072. The Arabs brought lemons and oranges, dates and cane sugar – significant exports to this day. During this golden era, Palermo was one of the wealthiest places in Europe. This is no longer the case, but Palermo remains a warm southern city with grand 18th-century architecture and much to recommend it.

Palermo is usually a full day's stay. It's pleasant to tour the sights in town in the morning, then spend the afternoon in the cool hills above, visiting the historic cathedral of Monreale. Organised cruise tours of both Palermo and Monreale are available, but each is easy to navigate independently.

The dock is only a 10- or 15-minute walk from the Teatro Politeama Garibaldi. Horse carts decorated with bells and colourful ribbons give romantic rides, but be firm in negotiating the price first. Taxi drivers offer tours of the city, but check that the driver's English is up to it, and be ready to bargain.

Along Corso Vittorio Emanuelle, set behind formal gardens with cool fountains, is the **Duomo** (cathedral; open Mon–Sat 9.30am–5.30pm; free). Further along the busy Corso Emanuelle, at Piazza Independenza, is the **Palazzo dei Normanni** (open Mon–Sat 9am–11.45am, Mon–Fri 3–4.45pm, Sun 9–10am, noon–12.45pm; admission fee). The palace houses the Parliament of Sicily, and mosaics and vaulted corridors of the interior give clues to its archaic grandeur. Quiet, shady gardens stretch in front of the palace.

The **Catacombe del Convento dei Cappuccini** (Capuchin Catacombs, Via Cappuccini; open Mon–Fri 9am–12pm, 1–5pm; admission fee) display the embalming skills of the Capuchin monks. This is not a visit for the faint-hearted. Mummified Palermitans lie in caskets and shelves, or stand in nooks along the walls. Congregated by sex, profession and age, the earthly remains of some 8,000 souls rest here.

Ships' excursions run to the remains of the ancient temples of **Selinunte** on the west coast, across a promontory. The town was all but destroyed in 410BC, but the remains indicate its prosperity and relative sophistication.

Monreale and Cefalù

Some cruises also offer tours to **Monreale**. (It's also possible to catch a bus from Piazza Independenza; the journey takes about 20 minutes, and it's easy to get a return taxi or bus from Monreale's Piazza Vittorio Emanuele.) This small, airy town in the cooler air of the hills has several shops, bars and pizzerias in which to while away the afternoon. The **Duomo** has the second-largest gold mosaic in antiquity – the larger one being in the Haghia Sophia mosque in Istanbul. Commenced in 1186, the interior is covered by 6,340 sq m (62,200 sq ft) of beautifully intricate Byzantine and Vene-

Monreale Cathedral

tian mosaics that illustrate biblical scenes and incorporate over a tonne of gold. As sunlight strikes through the high windows, the gold sparkles and radiates. The cathedral also has a fine Romanesque cloister. Other excursions include **Cefalù**, a pretty, medieval town with a Norman (Romanesque) cathedral, and a sandy beach. The town clings to a promontory around 60km (38 miles) east of Palermo.

Messina

Set on the Ionian Sea, but with a foothold in both the eastern and western Mediterranean, **Messina** has long been a key port of call. Rivalled only by Palermo and Catania, Messina is Sicily's cruising hub. However, an earthquake in 1908 flattened the area, so this is Sicily's least impressive coastal city. With little to detain visitors in the bland centre, the classic shore excursions glitter even more brightly. On offer are Taormina, Sicily's St-Tropez and its most dramatic resort; and an elemental excursion up **Mt Etna**, which normally obliges thrill-seekers with a display of smouldering volcanic activity. Neither experience should be missed, but if your spirit of adventure is dormant, then consider a stroll to view the Duomo, Messina's Norman cathedral, followed by a drink on the quayside.

> The treacherous waters of the Strait of Messina, separating Sicily from the Italian mainland, inspired the Greek myth of Scylla and Charybdis. Scylla, a six-headed beast who lived in rocks on the Italian side, devoured sailors, while Charybdis, a monster living in the whirlpool on the Sicilian side, took whole ships. We know now that the boisterous seas are simply the result of a clash between two currents that flow in opposite directions.

The lack of a dedicated cruise terminal at Messina is mired in regional politics, and darker forces cloud plans to build a vast bridge over the Strait of Messina. In the meantime, the port of Messina is a study in Sicilian chaos, even if the sail into the sweeping harbour suggests vestiges of the city's former grandeur. The sickle-shaped harbour can be very romantic at night, with the lights glittering on the waterfront.

In summer, a free tourist train meets passengers and sets off on a city centre tour. The tourist train tour includes the Norman **Duomo**, with an astronomical clock on its campanile, and several Arab-Norman churches that survived the earthquake. But unless you are feeling lazy, it is an easy stroll into the town centre.

Taormina
A spectacular location on the slopes of Monte Tauro overlooking the Bay of Giardini, with views west to Mt Etna

The Graeco-Roman theatre at Taormina

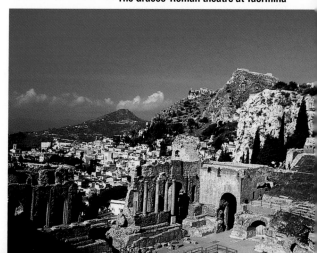

combined with atmospheric streets and bougainvillaea-decked courtyards have made **Taormina** popular with visitors down the centuries. Ships have to anchor off and tender into the jetty at the opposite end of the Bay of Giardini from Taormina. Cruise ships usually stay a full day.

You can see Taormina on the top of the hill overlooking the port of Giardini-Naxos as you arrive but, if your ship is leaving after dark, the departure is more spectacular as the city walls are illuminated at night. Most ships organise a shuttle bus into Taormina as well as trips to Mt Etna or half-day tours of the island. The journey into town takes around 15–20 minutes.

Almost immediately inside Porta Catania is the **Duomo**, and 5 minutes' walk further along smart Corso Umberto is **Piazza IX Aprile**, with spectacular views over the bay. About 5 minutes further on, Via Teatro Greco, to the right, leads almost immediately to the town's most popular attraction – the superbly sited **Teatro Greco-Romano** (Graeco-Roman Theatre; open daily 9am–5.30pm; admission fee), the third largest of its kind in the world. A tourist office, where train timetables are available, is housed in the **Museo Siciliano** (Sicilian Museum) at the junction with Via Teatre Greco. The station is a short walk away and there are frequent reasonably priced trains to Catania (1 hour away), Messina (70 minutes) and, less frequent, to Siracuse (2 hours 20 minutes).

Behind the tourist office, a steep road leads first to the castle and Sanctuary of the Madonna, then to the pretty village of **Castelmola** perched 3km (2 miles) above Taormina. The walk takes more than 2 hours so a lot of visitors prefer to take a taxi.

Catania

Although not without its problems – it's an industrial port, plagued by traffic chaos and crime, and the city's architecture has suffered over the years from earthquakes, eruptions from Mt Etna and World War II bombing – **Catania** does  have a certain crumbling charm.

Approaching the port on a clear day, **Mt Etna** can be seen smouldering behind the city. Not only is this volcano Sicily's greatest natural attraction, it is also its highest mountain. To the ancient Greeks, Mt Etna was the realm of Vulcan, god of fire, and home to the one-eyed Cyclops. It is Europe's highest – and also the world's oldest recorded – active volcano.

The main square, Piazza del Duomo, is only a stroll from the dock. It is the site of the 11th-century **Duomo**, which was re-modelled after a massive earthquake in the 17th century. The centrepiece of the square is the **Fontana dell'Elefante**, made from black lava. From here, head north up Via Etnea, the street where local people take their evening stroll, or *passeggiata*. Along this avenue are the best shops, cafés and boutiques.

Looking over Sicily , with Mt Etna in the foreground

Malta

Climate The climate of Malta has been the nation's fortune. Even in winter the temperature rarely drops below 12°C (54°F). Rain is likely to fall only between November and February. During the summer months it can top 43°C (109°F), although 29°C (84°F) is more usual. From April to September, there is virtually non-stop sunshine, plus soaring temperatures.

Time Zone GMT+1. From the last Sunday in March until the last Sunday in October, clocks are a further hour ahead of GMT.

Opening Times Banking hours are usually Monday–Friday 8.30am– 12.45pm; Saturday 8.30am–noon. Shops are generally open Monday–Friday 9am–7pm, with a long lunch break between 12.30pm and 4pm, and mornings only on Saturdays. In tourist resorts some shops may open throughout the day and at weekends.

What to Buy Maltese crafts include blown glass, Aran-style knitwear, lace, basketware and metalwork. Gold- and silverware are specialities.

Money Matters Maltese lira.

Festivals and Public Holidays 1 January, 10 February, 19, 31 March, Good Friday and Easter Day (March or April), 1 May, 7, 29 June, 15 August, 8, 21 September, 8, 13, 25 December.

Etiquette Women visiting churches must cover their shoulders and avoid plunging necklines, otherwise they may be handed a scarf to cover up, or refused entrance. A similar principle applies to men with shorts. Topless or nude sunbathing is against the law and punishable by fines, but both are customary on certain secluded beaches.

Tipping A 10 percent tip is usual for waiters. It is not necessary to tip taxi drivers.

Hazards and Security There is little violent crime and women need not feel unduly threatened when out alone at night. Common-sense precautions against bag snatchers or pickpockets should still taken.

Emergency Telephone Numbers Ambulance 196; fire and crime 199; traffic accidents 191.

Colourful boats in Valletta's harbour

MALTA

Malta has had more than its fair share of invaders, having been successively ruled by Phoenicia, Greece, Carthage, Rome, Arabs, Sicily, the Knights of St John of Jerusalem, France and eventually Britain until independence within the Commonwealth in 1964. It finally became a republic in 1974. The oval island, with neighbouring Gozo, is barely covered rock except for areas of market gardening, 'so dry that one expects oneself to begin to crackle', as D.H. Lawrence put it.

Valletta

Valletta has always displayed an implacable determination to repel invaders, which it matches with its elegant hospitality to visitors. Settlement on the site of the city can be dated back to the Bronze Age, and Mdina, the ancient capital, has a similarly long history; both are the principal destinations for cruise excursions. The capital city of

Malta, Valletta was founded in the 16th century, around the finest natural harbour in the Mediterranean, by the Knights of St John. After the Great Siege by the Turks in 1565, Jean de la Valletta had the town laid out and fortifications added. Francesco Laparelli, the Vatican architect, was responsible for the plan of streets in a regular grid relieved by open squares. French, Italian, Portuguese and Spanish Knights established *auberges* (inns) as residences, and these have been maintained and are open to view. The Knights held dominion over the island until Napoleon invaded and swept them away in 1798. Malta became a part of the British Empire two years later, and remained so until 1964.

Valletta's rooftops

Long known as a city built 'by gentlemen for gentlemen', Valletta's history is preserved with streets of splendid Renaissance and baroque architecture. The British past is still much in evidence and, while the Maltese now feel strongly about their own national identity, in some ways, the island feels more British than Britain.

Between the cloudless sky and the deep blue Mediterranean are the sheer cliffs and sheltering inlets of the northern Maltese coastline. The shoreline is broken by an impressive divided channel, guarded by Fort Ricasoli to the east and pierced by the bastions of Fort Saint Elmo, the northernmost fortification of Valletta.

The steep honey-coloured walls of Valletta rise behind and around the magnificent sweep of the Grand Harbour. The town makes a pleasing and orderly skyline, punctuated by occasional towers and domes. It's worth making it out on deck to observe the arrival, or choosing a table with a decent view

Malta is renowned for its fresh fish

when having breakfast. This is most likely to be forward on the starboard side, but ask a waiter at dinner the night before.

The boat docks at a wide quay, south of Grand Harbour, set aside for cruise liners. The quay is lined with excursion buses and shuttles, and surrounded by old maritime buildings, many of which are being renovated or replaced.

The town is about 15–20 minutes' walk away from the port, and the walk is hot, dusty and rather steep. Taxis are not expensive, and you should be aware that while officials try to get you to buy tickets before leaving the harbour gates, once beyond the gates there are numerous taxis vying for custom. Water taxis also run from the harbour.

City Sights

Once you are in town, Valletta is made for walking. There are also taxis, if you want them, and horse-drawn carriages – *karrozzini*. Be sure to negotiate a price before taking a ride. Streets are wide and comfortable, characterised by squat palm trees, and distances are short. Handsome, pale-stone façades are lined with regular green balconies and shutters.

Valletta has many fine churches and museums, spectacular, airy gardens and spacious outdoor cafés.

In Palace Square (Misrah San Gorg), the **Grand Master's Palace** (open Oct–mid-Jun Mon–Sat 8.15am–5pm, Sun 8.15am–4.15pm, mid-Jun–Sept Mon–Sun 7.45am–2pm: admission fee) was built for the founding Knights in 1580, and has artwork and trimmings to prove it. The Maltese Parliament sits in the armoury hall, the separate museum has a fine display of armour, including a gold-plated set, and the tapestry chamber is where the Knights' Council was formerly convened.

Walk up Old Theatre Street to the **Manoel Theatre** (tours Mon–Fri 10.30am and 11.30am, Sat 11.30am only; admission fee includes admission to the theatre museum). Founded in 1731, this is where the Knights not only were entertained, but gave performances themselves. Reputedly the second-

The Basilica of Our Lady of Mt Carmel

oldest theatre in use in Europe, the auditorium is finely featured with gilded boxes and an ornate ceiling.

The restored **Basilica of Our Lady of Mt Carmel** (1570) is adjacent to the Manoel Theatre. The domed basilica was bombed during World War II, when strategic Valletta suffered badly, but it was meticulously reconstructed in the 1950s.

Return to Palace Square and to the right along Republic Street, on St John's

St John's Co-Cathedral knocker

Square, is **St John's Co-Cathedral** (open Mon–Fri, Sat am only, Sun services only; free). Sir Walter Scott called the spectacular baroque interior of 1577 the most striking he had ever seen. Modest dress is required.

In the Auberge de Provence is the **National Museum of Archaeology** (open Oct–mid-Jun Mon–Sat 8.15am–5pm, Sun 8.15am–4.15pm, mid-Jun–Sept Mon–Sun 7.45am–2pm; admission fee). The *auberge* itself is sumptuous, and the museum is an interesting bonus, displaying pottery, statuettes, stone implements, jewellery and other artefacts from the island's prehistory.

At the far (sea) end of Valletta is **Fort St Elmo**, site of the Knights' original fortification, and home of the **National War Museum** (open Oct–mid-Jun Mon–Sat 8.15am–5pm, Sun 8.15am–4.15pm, mid-Jun–Sept Mon–Sun 7.45am–2pm: admission fee). The World War II exhibits make clear why the whole island of Malta was awarded the George Cross for its bravery and resilience in that conflict. High above the town sit the **Upper Barracca Gardens** (open daily, 7am–6pm; free), which offer a panoramic view.

Shopping is pleasant, as many of the stores are beautifully decorated. Local specialities include lace and embroidery, ceramics and glassware. The street market along Merchant Street, starting at Market Square is particularly good.

Excursions from Valletta are usually organised to several towns on Malta, notably Mdina and Vittoriosa.

Mdina

In the centre of the island lies **Mdina**, Malta's medieval capital, which can trace its origins back more than 4,000 years. The narrow streets and high vantage point (150m/500ft above sea level) made it easy to defend, and also allows it to take the best advantage of the breezes in summer. You enter the old city via a small bridge and a splendid arch. Among

Aerial view of the town of Mdina and its neighbouring village Rabat

many lovely buildings, quite a few of which date from a 17th-century reconstruction after an earthquake, is the **Cathedral**, which has beautiful mosaics and marble tombs. There are cruise excursions here, but Mdina can also be reached by bus from Valletta. Whether you go alone or on a tour, be aware that there is quite a lot of walking involved.

Vittoriosa

There are cruise excursions to **Vittoriosa**, too, but it is very close to Valletta and can easily be reached by bus, or by taxi. Also known as Birgu, this 16th-century walled city may be worth a visit if you have time. One advantage of the cruise excursion is that it includes a trip across the Grand Harbour on a traditional Maltese *dhajsa* – the brightly coloured boats with 'eyes' painted on the prow –

The Eyes of Osiris

All traditional fishing boats in Maltese waters have an eye painted on each side of their bow. These eyes of Osiris, the pagan god of fertility and of the dead, ward off any evil that may be out at sea. On this staunchly Catholic island, he's in the company of saints, as most boats are named after saints and carry shrines. Every spring, before the fishermen put their boats on the water for the summer, they will paint the eyes afresh to give them maximum protection.

but these trips, too, can be negotiated at the harbour.

Boating, jet-skiing and scuba-diving opportunities are included on shore excursions, but these beaches, too, are only a very short distance from Valletta. If you want to go it alone, trips are quite easy to arrange once you are ashore.

Croatia

Climate The Adriatic coast has a more Mediterranean climate than the rest of the country, with hot, sunny summer days and mild, wet winters. Coastal temperatures are around 5–10°C (40–50°F) in January and reach highs of 30°C (86°F) in August. The tourist season is April–October.

Time Zone GMT+1.

Opening Times Banks are generally open 7am–3pm Monday–Friday and 8am–2pm on Saturday. Shops are open from 8am–7/8pm Monday–Friday and 8am–2pm on Saturday. Shops in some tourist resorts open 8am–1pm and 5–11pm.

What to Buy Traditional Croatian souvenirs include hand-made silk ties and lace, fragrant herbal remedies (especially lavender), stone-ware and glassware.

Money Matters The currency is the kuna (100 lipa make 1 kuna), but euros are widely accepted.

Festivals and Public Holidays 1, 6 January, Easter, 1 May, Corpus Christi, 22, 25 June, 5, 15 August, 8 October, 1 November, 25 and 26 December.

Etiquette As Croatia is a religious country with a Roman Catholic major-ity, public displays of affection between homosexuals are unwelcome.

Tipping Tax and service are usually included in hotel and restaurant bills, but it is customary to round up the amount to the nearest 10 kunas. Taxi drivers routinely round up the fare, so no tip is necessary.

Hazards and Security A sun hat and sunscreen are necessary in summer. Bathers should beware of sea urchins, black spiky balls about the size of a child's fist. If trodden on, a sea urchin's spines can become painfully implanted in the skin.

Drugs and Medicines Citizens of the UK and most European countries are entitled to free medical care thanks to a mutual health agreement. Ask at post offices in the UK for the relevant forms.

Emergency Telephone Numbers Police 92.

Church bells in Croatia

CROATIA

Since the end of the four-year war against Serbia that followed the break-up of Yugoslavia in 1991 and the creation of an independent Croatia, the country has been working hard to rebuild its tourist industry. With 2,000km (1,250 miles) of coastline and approximately 1,000 islands, Croatia has great appeal for cruise ships. The principal cruise ports lie on the Dalmatian coast: Split, Croatia's second city, which has outstanding Roman remains; the World Heritage site of Dubrovnik, with an entirely pedestrianised historic core within the medieval walls; and the islands of Korcula and well-forested Hvar.

Split

Situated on the sunny Dalmatian coast of Croatia, **Split** is one of the Adriatic's liveliest and most alluring cities. Arriving here on a cruise ship and catching sight of its old town shimmering in the morning light against a backdrop of sheer lime-

Croatian dishes worth trying include *lignje* (fried squid), *pasticada* (stuffed roast beef) and *ćevapčići* (spicy meat-balls). The local Merlot is excellent and you can round off your meal with a glass of Dubrovnik firewater, Travarica, which is pleasantly flavoured with herbs.

stone mountains creates a memorable first impression. The port is situated right in the centre of the city, with the heart of the old quarter within 200m/yds or five minutes' walk. The railway station is even closer (100m/yds).

The palm-fringed waterfront **Riva** is lined with pavement cafés and cheap restaurants. From here you can head straight into **Dioklecijanova palača** (Diocletian's Palace) through the bronze gate, which used to be right on the water's edge and accessible only by boat. The centre of Split life still focuses upon the palace, built by the Roman emperor Diocletian as a retirement home between AD295 and 305. Over 200 buildings, and around 3,000 residents remain inside the original complex: the old chambers and garrisons have been converted over the centuries into shops, bars, cafés and hotels as well as ordinary homes. **Sv Duje Katedrala** (Cathedral of St Domnius; open Mon–Sat 7am–12pm, 4–7pm, Sun 11am–12pm; free), whose lofty bell tower is one of the symbols of the city, was a 13th-century addition. The palace is a UNESCO World Heritage site.

Excursions from Split

The customary half-day tour from Split is to the once-thriving Roman town of **Salona**, around 5km (3 miles) away. Diocletian was born near here, and it was on account of his affection for the place that he built his palatial home in nearby Split. As the attacks of the Slavs in the 7th century took their toll on Salona, the citizens fled to Diocletian's Palace, thus ensuring its survival and the life that still bustles within its stone walls. A number of remains dot the landscape of Salona, and it is possible to trace the original shape of the city and various structures, such as the amphitheatre that in its heyday played host to a baying crowd of 18,000.

Dubrovnik

George Bernard Shaw described **Dubrovnik** as 'paradise on earth', and visitors to this supremely beautiful 12th-century walled city will certainly agree. The old town – now largely recovered from the shelling it received during the civil war of 1991 – is crammed with architectural wonders and offers fabulous views of the Adriatic coast from its high ramparts. There are more delights just along the coast in the form of lovely countryside, stunning sea views and attractive traditional villages.

UNESCO-protected Dubrovnik, jewel of the Dalmatian coast

Dubrovnik is a popular port of call on Mediterranean itineraries, and ships spend a full day and sometimes an evening here to allow passengers plenty of time to explore. While some ships tender passengers into the old harbour in the heart of Dubrovnik's old town, most berth in the main dock at the end of the waterfront marina and provide shuttle buses for the 10-minute drive to the old town's **Vrata Pile** (pronounced *Pee-lay*) – Pile Gate. If you're feeling active, walk to the old centre – it's a pretty route, but uphill.

Just to the right as you leave the dock is a pretty harbour filled with colourful boats, some of which offer lunch and dinner cruises. A little further along, there's a colourful flower and vegetable market held daily.

Refreshing friendships in a Dubrovnik café

If you're dropped off in Pile Square, take a moment to walk to the waterfront balustrade to enjoy the magnificent harbour view before strolling down the ramps into the old city.

The first thing to greet you as you enter via Pile Gate is the imposing **Onofrijeva česma** (Onofrio's Fountain), one of Dubrovnik's most famous landmarks, which was constructed in the 1430s as part of an elaborate system of aqueducts and canals designed to carry water to the city from a well 12km (8 miles) beyond its walls. Right

ahead of you now is Placa
Stradun. Immediately to your
left, though, is the 14th-cen-
tury **Franjevački samostan**
(Franciscan Monastery; open
daily, 9am–6pm; admission
fee), and you should explore

**Wear sensible shoes
when touring Dubrovnik
as the cream marble
paving of the Placa
Stradun, although spec-
tacular, can be slippery.**

here first, as its cloister is exquisite, and was one of the few
places to survive the catastrophic earthquake that ravaged
Dubrovnik in 1667; the rest of the monastery collapsed and
was rebuilt. Of particular interest here is a beautiful statue of
the Pietá, carved in 1498, and the world's oldest pharmacy,
established in 1391.

Walk to the other end of the *placa* and you'll find the only
other building to have survived the 1667 earthquake, the
magnificent **Palača Sponza** (Sponza Palace; open daily,
7am–2pm; free), which is notable for its elaborate curved
portico and Gothic windows. The palace now houses the
state archives of Dubrovnik and also contains a small maritime museum and art gallery. Just beyond it, through a stone
archway, is the old harbour, while if you head right and cross
Puljana Luza, you'll find the baroque, 18th-century **Sv
Vlaha**, or Church of St Blaise, Dubrovnik's patron saint. His
remains are in Dubrovnik's **Katedrala Velike Gospe**
(Cathedral of the Assumption of the Virgin; open Mon–Sat
8am–8pm, Sun 11am–5.30pm; admission fee), which lies
behind the church. The cathedral also contains a stunning
collection of gold and silver medieval reliquaries. Just off
Puljana Luza is a paved square where a craft market is held
most mornings; good buys are embroidery and lace,
flavoured oils and lavender products.

Go left past the Sponza Palace to reach the 14th-century
Dominikanski samostan (Dominican Monastery; open
daily 9am–6pm; admission fee), which houses a collection

of religious art and artefacts from the 14th and 15th centuries, and has a lovely cloister.

If it's your first time in Dubrovnik, make time for a walk around the **fortified walls**, which offer panoramic views of the old city. The entrance to the walls is just inside Pile Gate, so you could start or end your tour here. And if that leaves you in need of fortification yourself, you'll find plenty of restaurants tucked away in the alleys of Dubrovnik, as well as lively (if a little more expensive) outdoor cafés on the main streets.

Tours outside Dubrovnik usually feature the scenic coastline, sometimes pausing at a village for a wine-tasting before visiting the resort of Cavatt.

Hvar

Hvar, the main settlement on the Croatian island of the same name, is visited mainly by smaller ships. Make the most of

Hvar rooftops

your time there, as some cruise ships do not stay long enough for more than a four-hour excursion round the island or shorter tour of the town, which is a shame, as the traffic-free medieval town is lovely.

Cruise passengers tender into Hvar's pretty harbour, which is lined with shops, cafés and hotels. Turn right from the harbour and you'll find the town's huge, marble-paved piazza with more shops and bars. Go left instead and you'll find more

A favourite activity in Hvar is to take a 'Fish Picnic' cruise

shops and cafés and travel agencies selling wine tours, island tours and 'Fish Picnic' cruises at affordable prices. In the summer months, a water taxi operates from the harbour to the island's main beaches, and boats can be hired for fishing trips.

The main town of Hvar was a naval base for the Venetian fleet from the 12th to the 18th century, and the Venetians have left their mark: the pedestrian-only, marble-paved streets shimmer as though filled with water; a well-preserved walled fortress overlooks the harbour; and the town's main square, **Trg Sv Stjepana** – originally a water-filled inlet that was reclaimed by the inhabitants in the 16th century – is the largest piazza in all of Dalmatia. In the centre is an ornate well constructed in 1520, and the square is dominated by the **Katedrala Sv Stjepana** (Cathedral of St Stephen), which has a remarkable Venetian bell tower.

Above the square, just beneath the 13th-century ramparts, are the remains of grand Gothic palaces once occupied by

Hvar's aristocracy. The narrow (and unnamed) streets of the town are well worth exploring.

Also worth seeing is the large **arsenal** (its vast arches now occupied by shops), which was built in 1611 to repair, refit and equip war galleons. At its northern end – an area that was once a food store – a theatre was installed in 1612 with a pit for the commoners and boxes for the gentry.

The island has a lovely coastline and is well-wooded and lush with typical Mediterranean vegetation and wild lavender fields (for which the island is famed). It is dotted with historical monuments and ancient settlements such as the 2nd-century BC village of **Starigrad**; Starigrad, sited on a beautiful bay, has a Dominican monastery, which houses a priceless collection of paintings and manuscripts.

If you just want to laze on a beach, you could consider taking a boat from the harbour at Hvar to the **Pakleni Islets**, just a short distance – the pick of the bunch is probably the nearest, **Jerolim**. Alternatively, just walk along the coast east of town to reach a series of small coves with pebble beaches.

Korčula

The long, thin island of Korčula hangs off the edge of the Pelješac Peninsula. **Korčula Town** is the main attraction, a

---

Moreška Dance

Korčula is the birthplace of Croatia's traditional dance, the Moreška, dating from the 15th century. A predictable story of good and evil, it dramatises the battle of two kings, the white and the black, who fight to woo the favours of a fair maiden. Performances (Monday and Thursday in high season) are held in the small outdoor theatre in Korčula Town. The most important Moreška of the year is performed on 27 July on the feast of St Theodore.

The Dalmatian coast is one the most beautiful in the Mediterranean

chocolate-box ensemble of orange-hued roofs and spires. The town plan is straightforward and makes walking around easy – the main thoroughfare runs right through the heart of the old centre and a waterside boulevard circles the peninsula. Only the smaller cruise ships call in at Korčula, docking conveniently right in the centre of town.

The town's most striking building is **Katedrala Sv Marka** (St Mark's Cathedral), a triple-naved basilica with an impressive interior containing an *Annunciation* by Tintoretto, who spent time in Korčula as a student. The **town museum** (open high season: Mon–Sat 9am–1pm and 5–7pm; low season: 9am–1pm; admission fee), which has a small art gallery and exhibits related to maritime history, is housed in an impressive 16th-century palace. There are several bathing **beaches** around the town – a couple near the Marco Polo Hotel and many more less crowded ones near the town of **Lumbarda** to the south and also at **Blato**, a pleasant village to the west.

Greece

Climate Athens has short, cold winters and long, dry and hot summers. There can be considerable variation between the islands: the Ionian Islands are cooler and wetter than Crete or Rhodes. The shoulders of the summer season require warm clothes and rainwear.

Time Zone GMT+2.

Opening Times Business and shopping hours vary according to the type of business and the day of the week. If you are after something important, the hours between 10am and 1pm Monday–Friday are the only hours when everything is guaranteed to be open. Many shops take a long lunch break, then open again in the late afternoon. Only in Athens are the hours more typical of other EU countries: non-food shops are likely to be open Monday–Wednesday 9am–5pm, Tuesday, Thursday–Friday 10am–7pm, Saturday 8.30am–3.30pm.

What to Buy Brightly coloured ceramics, leather sandals and bags, silver jewellery, sponges, wild herbs and olive oil.

Money Matters Euro.

Festivals and Public Holidays 1, 6 January, Shrove Monday (48 days before Easter), 25 March, Good Friday and Greek Orthodox Easter, Pentecost Monday (50 days after Easter), 1 May, 15 August, 28 October, 25, 26 December.

Etiquette Nude bathing is legal on very few Greek beaches, and some people ignoring the ban have become acquainted with Greek jails.

Tipping Most restaurants and tavernas include a 15 percent service charge in menu prices, so a tip is not expected, although it is customary to round up by leaving the small change.

Hazards and Security Crime is rare on the islands, and the petty thieving that does occur might well be carried out by other tourists. Special officers known as tourist police are assigned to help tourists on some islands; they usually speak some English.

Emergency Telephone Numbers Ambulance 166; police 100; tourist police (Athens) 171.

Sublime Santoríni

GREECE

With more than 50 inhabited islands, it is little wonder that Greece has had a long attachment to the sea and shipping. The beauty and proximity of many of the Greek islands makes it a natural cruise destination, since cruising among islands is more appealing than open water to the horizon. All lie in the Aegean Sea except the Ionian Islands, the westernmost cluster in the sea of the same name; the principal cruise islands are Corfu and Zákynthos. The largest group lies to the east of the Peloponnese: the Cyclades are characterised by their white houses and fabulous beaches as well as important archaeological sites, such as Apollo's ancient Delos on Mýkonos. Dramatic Santoríni is visited by many cruise ships for its extraordinary volcanic bay. Finally the Dodecanese include Rhodes and Kós, two popular destinations. Athens (Piraeus) and the ports of the Peloponnese also feature in most eastern Mediterranean itineraries.

MAINLAND GREECE

Mainland Greece has more than enough to offer the visitor, from the history and nightlife of Athens, to the temples and treasures of nearby sites such as Delphi and Epidaurus and, further afield, the archaeological wonders of the Peloponnese.

Piraeus (Athens)

The decision to stage the summer Olympic Games in Athens in 2004 ensured a frenzied clean-up, with tree-planting and landscaping, new buildings and restorations galore. Although new tram lines were built, traffic and pollution remain a problem, but Athens is a compulsive metropolis that has attracted and enthralled visitors for centuries.

Piraeus (Pireás), the port for Athens, is frequently used as a starting point for cruises. All cruise ships, whether home-porting or visiting, dock alongside rather than anchoring off.

Pheidias' masterpiece, the Parthenon

Arriving by ship you may see the imposing Temple of Poseidon perched on Cape Sounion to the southeast; once in the approaches to Piraeus, however, it will be the marine traffic that catches your eye. One of the busiest ports in the Mediterranean, Piraeus receives over 12 million ferry and cruise visitors every year, so ships are coming and going all the time.

Taxis meet all visiting cruise ships but the traffic in Piraeus and Athens is always

Odeion of Herodus Atticus

heavy so, instead of a stop-start, 10-km (6-mile) journey of at least 30 minutes into central Athens, an excellent option is to take the metro rail service to the main city sights. The station (on Aktí Miaoúli) is set back from the harbour and is a longish walk from the cruise ship dock, so ships usually offer a shuttle service (free or small charge). There is only one metro line from Piraeus so it is difficult to go wrong – the main stations are Omónia (one of the two most important squares in Athens), Thisío (for the Acropolis) and Monastiráki (for Pláka). Although there are a couple of good museums in Piraeus (archaeological and maritime) and some cafés and restaurants, there is no reason to linger here for long when Athens, Cape Sounion and the Corinth Canal are close by.

Athens

The 'High City', the **Acropolis** (open Mon–Fri 8am– 4.30pm, Sat–Sun 8.30am–2.30pm; admission fee) is the prime attraction with the 4th-century BC **Parthenon**, temple to Athena, the

Odeion of Herodus Atticus and the Theatre of Dionysos. The previously traffic-clogged road of Dionysíou Areopagítou around the base of the Acropolis has been pedestrianised. With the Parthenon towering overhead, it quickly established itself as a popular place for the evening *vólta*, or stroll.

The 2nd-century **Hadrian's Arch** is one of several other historic sites nearby. It once marked the point where the Classical Greek city ended and the Roman town began. Close by stand the towering columns of the **Temple of Olympian Zeus**. In the other direction, just north of the Acropolis, is the well-preserved, marble Roman Tower of the Winds.

The Temple of Olympian Zeus stands at the south end of the **National Gardens**. At the gardens' far end is **Platía Sýntagma** – Constitution Square – home to the Tomb of the Unknown Soldier and the former royal palace, now the main parliament building, which is guarded by the soldiers whose traditional dress and high-stepping marches have fascinated visitors down the years. Down from Sýntagma (at Amalías 26) is the office of the GNTO (Greek National Tourism Organisation).

Athens really has to be seen in sections; the centre is too large (and usually too crowded) to be walked properly without using some form of transport between the

The view from Lykavitós

major sights. The new tram
system runs along the sea
from Fáliro to Glyfáda with a
line into the city centre at
Sýntagma. Buses are cheap
but crowded and slow and it
can be difficult to work out
where they are going. The
three lines of the metro are
the best way to get around,
simple to negotiate and fast,
and there are stations near the
most important sights.

**Golden Mask of Agamemnon,
National Archaeological Museum**

Although not particularly
interesting or attractive, **Platía Omónias** (Omónia Square,
reached by metro directly from Piraeus) is a good focal point
as it stands at the edge of the city's main shopping district
and is close to the **National Archaeological Museum** (open
Mon 12.30–7pm, Tues–Fri 8am–7pm, Sat–Sun 8.30am–
3pm; admission fee).

If you went directly by metro to Omónia from Piraeus,
you could board it again to **Monastiráki**, from which it is
about 10–15 minutes' walk along Ermoú – a pleasant, pedestrianised street – to Sýntagma, and about the same distance
to Pláka and the Acropolis.

From Sýntagma you can walk east along Vasilísis Sofías to
reach three excellent museums – the **Goulandris Museum**
(open Tues–Thur, Sat–Sun 9am–2pm; admission fee) with a
collection of beautiful Cycladic idols; the **Benaki Museum**
(open Tues–Sun 8.30am–3pm; admission fee), with two icons
attributed to El Greco; and the **Byzantine Museum** (hours as
for Benaki), its treasures housed in a Florentine-style mansion.

Besides Athens itself, excursions commonly include the
Corinth Canal, Mycenae and Epidaurus *(see page 166)*.

Itéa (Delphi)

Built on the Gulf of Corinth and surrounded by olive groves, **Itéa** is a pleasant little port used as a gateway to Delphi, possibly Greece's most famous and magical classical site.

Cruise ships either tender or dock at the pier near the town centre. There's not a great deal in the modern town itself, as everything is geared towards visiting Delphi. If you don't want to visit the site, you will find pretty tavernas along the waterfront and some decent swimming beaches nearby.

Delphi (open Mon–Fri 7.30am–6.30pm, Sat–Sun 8.30am–3pm) is around 20 minutes away by bus or taxi, on the slopes of craggy **Mt Parnassós**, looking out over the olive groves stretching all the way to the coast. It's a good idea, particularly if you are visiting without a guide, to go first to the **museum** (open daily 9am–3pm; admission fee; combined ticket with Sanctuary of Apollo available), which gives a better perspective on the region's turbulent history.

Temple of Athena Pronaia at Delphi

Delphi was revered by the ancient Greeks as the sanctuary of Apollo and the home of his oracle, which brought pilgrims from all over the ancient world to seek advice. It was also the site of the Pythian Games, held every four years and included musical, literary and athletic contests.

The Peloponnese

The Peloponnese takes its name from the legendary hero Pelops, plus the Greek for island, *nísos*, although it is seldom thought of as an island. An incredible variety of Classical, medieval and later sights can be found here.

Katákolo (Olympia)

The small Ionian port of **Katákolo**, on the Peloponnesian mainland, is used mostly as a base from which to visit ancient Olympia, the sanctuary of Zeus and site of the first Olympic Games (776BC). It is here that the Olympic torch is lit. The games were held every four years at full moon in August or September after the harvest, and drew thousands of spectators from all over the ancient world.

There is not much of interest in Katákolo, and almost all visitors head straight for Olympia, 48km (30 miles) inland. Here you'll find a handful of bars and tavernas, and shops selling Olympic memorabilia, souvenirs, statues, leather items and jewellery.

It's best to join a shore excursion to **Olympia**, although there are taxis. The site is set in forests of pine and oak and is still being excavated – it was discovered in 1766 under several metres of mud. It was almost destroyed by forest fires in 1998 but fortunately survived.

Today, you can see the Roman baths, the massive gymnasium, where the athletes trained, the **stadium** (open daily 8am–7pm; admission fee), the Temples of Zeus and his wife, Hera, a Roman swimming pool, Roman fountains and the workshop of Phidias, who built a vast gold and ivory statue of Zeus that was considered one of the Seven Wonders of the Ancient World and was housed in the temple of Zeus.

The bronze, marble and terracotta statues in the **Archaeological Museum** (open Mon 12–7pm, Tues–Sun 8am–7pm; admission fee) are stunning and there's lots of fascinating memorabilia from the ancient games, including weights and discuses. More souvenirs are in the **Museum of the Olympic Games** (open Mon 12–7pm, Tues–Sun 8am–7pm; admission fee) in the town, 15 minutes' walk from the ancient site.

Gýthio (Mystrás)

The ancient port of **Gýthio**, on the southern coast of the Peloponnese, was founded by the Phoenecians around 400BC, and for centuries served as the port for Sparta, some 50km (30 miles) to the north. Nowadays the town is a holiday resort and a deceptively congenial gateway to the austere Máni peninsula. Most cruise passengers calling in at Gýthio take the tour to Sparta and Mystrás.

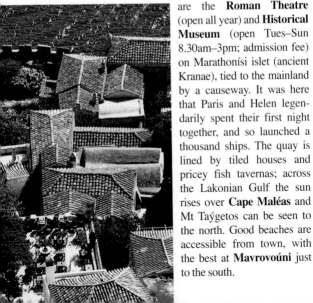

Peloponnesian rooftops

The main sights in Gýthio are the **Roman Theatre** (open all year) and **Historical Museum** (open Tues–Sun 8.30am–3pm; admission fee) on Marathonísi islet (ancient Kranae), tied to the mainland by a causeway. It was here that Paris and Helen legendarily spent their first night together, and so launched a thousand ships. The quay is lined by tiled houses and pricey fish tavernas; across the Lakonian Gulf the sun rises over **Cape Maléas** and Mt Taýgetos can be seen to the north. Good beaches are accessible from town, with the best at **Mavrovoúni** just to the south.

The most rewarding excursion inland is to **Mystrás**, 6km (4 miles) to the west: a city of 20,000 under Byzantine rule in medieval times, it remains remarkably complete to this day – a romantically ruined walled town clinging to a conical crag and topped by a castle.

There is not a great deal to see at **Sparta** (Spartí); the ruins of the ancient city, Athens' rival in Classical times, are thin on the ground, although the small archaeological museum (open Tues–Sun 9am–5pm; admission fee) is excellent.

Navplio (Nafplion)

Návplio (Nafplion) was Greece's first capital after the Greek War of Independence (1821–28) against the Ottoman Empire. Today, this attractive town serves as a base for day trips to the ancient site at Epídavros *(see page 166)*, as well as to Mycenae and Corinth.

Návplio is a tender port, and passengers are usually dropped in the busy harbour, close to the walkable town, which has shady parks, stepped side streets and lots of small churches and museums. Don't miss the **mosque** off Platía Sýntagma (Constitution Square) where Greece's first parliament met, or the elegant neoclassical civic buildings.

The best shops are on Staïkopoúlou, immediately above Platía Sýndagma, and Vas. Konstantínou, which runs parallel to it. Best buys include jewellery, icons, antiques, shadow puppets, worry beads, Greek wine and honey.

Návplio has two hilltop fortresses and a miniature castle on an island in the harbour, exploration of which could easily fill a day. **Akronavpliá** fortress was begun in Byzantine times and finished in the late 17th century, about the same time that the Venetian **Palamídi** was built. There are said to be 999 steps up the rock face, which you can climb to the latter, but it's easier to take a taxi to both fortresses, especially in hot weather. The views from the top are breathtaking, with the town spilling

> The word 'currant'
> derives from 'Corinth',
> a reference to the city's
> long-established trade
> in dried grapes, still
> one of Greece's most
> successful exports.

away below and the little 15th-century **Boúrtzi Castle** squatting on its island in the harbour. The castle can be reached by a short motorboat trip for a couple of euros.

Excursions from Návplio

The principal destination of excursions from Návplio is the magnificent 4th-century BC amphitheatre at **Epídavros**, 27km (17 miles) to the east. It is a party piece of tour guides to illustrate the perfect acoustics of the 14,000-seat theatre by either dropping a coin or singing a solo while the group sit in the uppermost seats. Astonishingly, this vast structure was discovered and excavated as recently as the 19th century. Built of white limestone, the theatre has 54 tiers of seats and a wonderful backdrop of hills. It was used for plays that were part of a quadrennial festival following the Isthmian games. Besides the theatre, the site includes a museum and the remains of the Asklepian sanctuary, which was renowned for healing. The functions of the buildings are understood and clearly labelled.

Also nearby is **Mycenae**, home to some impressive excavations dating back to 1250BC. There are further excavations in **Corinth**, including the 6th-century BC Temple of Apollo.

Thessaloníki

⚓ **Thessaloníki** (sometimes referred to as Salonika in the West) is the capital of the ancient region of Macedonia and the second most important city in Greece. It is very much a sophisticated town with a distinctive character, excellent restaurants, a decent collection of Roman ruins and fabulous Byzantine churches. Founded in 316BC by Philip II of Macedon, father of Alexander the Great, Thessaloníki became part of the Roman Empire in 168BC. Thessaloníki is a port of call on Aegean, Greece/Turkey and Black Sea itineraries. The port is a 200m (yds) walk from the city centre.

The 15th-century **White Tower** (Lefkós Pýrgos) is the city's symbol. A good place to get an overview of the city's colourful history, is the **Byzantine Museum**, as is the **Archaeological Museum**, both of which lie north of the tower, opposite the Exhibition Grounds (both open daily; admission fee).

After lunch in one of the appetising restaurants you could visit the stunning, 3rd-century **Rotunda of Ághios Geórgios** at the top of Goúnari, built as a Roman mausoleum and converted to a church by Constantine the Great, the first Christian Roman emperor; or take a short taxi ride to **Kástra**, the city's atmospheric Turkish quarter and the only part of 19th-century Thessaloníki to survive the earthquake and fire that devastated the city in 1917.

Café on Thessaloníki's waterfront

THE ISLANDS

The poet Odysseus Elytis once said: 'Greece rests on the sea.' It's an observation that few countries could claim with such authority. Some 25,000 sq km (10,000 sq miles) of the Aegean and Ionian seas are covered by islands. And, in characteristic Greek fashion, the exact number of them has been the topic of discussion and dispute. There may be 3,000 islands and islets, of which 167 are inhabited. Or, according to someone else's calculations, there may be only 1,000, of which fewer than 60 are populated. Here, for ease of reference, we've organised them by island groups.

The Ionian Islands

Lushest of all the Greek island chains, the Ionians offer superb beaches, great natural beauty and a distinct culture, including a graceful Venetian influence in the local architecture.

Corfu (Kerkyra)

⚓ **Corfu** (Kérkyra) is one of the largest of the Greek islands and has become a popular holiday destination because of its sunny climate, sandy beaches and relaxed lifestyle. Cruise visitors arrive conveniently close to **Corfu Town** (Kérkyra Town) where the old quarter, with its cobblestone streets and alleyways, historic buildings, statues and fountains, is the largest preserved medieval town in Greece that is still fully inhabited and functional. The Venetians, French and British have all had an influence on the architecture, and the old (Venetian) fortress jutting out from the coast road is a UNESCO World Heritage site. Beyond the old town, the island offers many attractive drives through pine woods, a variety of beach resorts and small inland villages where time appears to have stood still.

Cruise lines occasionally home-port ships here – the airport is only a few kilometres from the port/Corfu Town – and offer

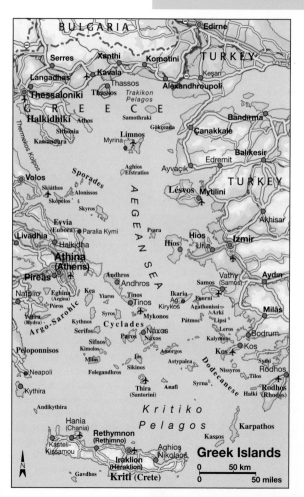

Greek Islands

the cruise combined with a stay on the island. But mostly it serves as a port of call, with ships usually staying a full day.

There is nothing much to see as you arrive at the island's busy commercial and naval port and it is usually a 5- to 10-minute walk just to get from the ship to the dock entrance where there is a ferry ticket office (ferries go to Igoumenítsa on the Greek mainland) along with some public telephones and a small exchange bureau. Most ships offer a free (or cheap) shuttle into the old town. This will take you past a market, around the outer edge of town, dropping off across the park from Listón Arcade. If you decide to walk into the old town, it's quicker via the coast road – approximately

Backstreets in Corfu Town

1km (less than a mile) and around 15 minutes from the dock gates. But there's not much to see along the way so it's probably best to take the shuttle and start walking when in town.

There is a fish, food and clothes market inside the old town walls at the Venetian gates. Otherwise, the main shopping area is behind Listón Arcade and esplanade. One of the best buys is olive wood that has been carved into bowls, bread boards or statues. Leather, furs, jewellery and colourful ceramics are also worth a look. A few shops close in the afternoon but most stay open all day.

Corfu Old Town is compact and easily walkable even if you take taxis (which come to where the ships dock) or a shuttle bus there and back. Roads are too narrow and the traffic too heavy to make any other kind of transport a better option. Take care though: streets are uneven and full of potholes. Watch out, too, for the traffic: even where pavements exist, local drivers are quite willing to use them as a quick way through the traffic.

An elegant Corfiote

Road and street signs are usually given in Greek and in transliteration, but may differ a little from the Greek or transliteration used on town maps provided by the ship or locally. The maps are not generally very reliable and it is easy to get lost if you try to follow them closely. However, most local people speak enough English to direct you.

Likely destinations will probably include the 16th-century **Ághios Spyrídon Church** – its red-domed belfry stands out just behind Listón Arcade; and the 19th-century **Palace of St Michael and St George** on the other side of the esplanade. Its east wing houses the **Museum of Asiatic Art** (open Tues–Sun 8.30am–3pm; admission fee), which has one of the largest private collections of Asiatic art in the world. Around the back (on the Old Fort side), set in lovely gardens, is the **Municipal Art Gallery** (open daily 9am–5pm; admission fee).

The **Archaeological Museum** (open Tues–Sun 8.30am–3pm; admission fee) in Vraíla Street has some pieces dating back to Roman times and retrieved from local excavations.

For a drink or lunch, choose one of the cafés along Listón Arcade, which was designed by the French to echo the Parisian rue de Rivoli, and looks out over the park in front of the Old Fort – reputedly the largest open square in Greece. There are better cafés elsewhere but these have the best views.

Excursions on Corfu may include horse-drawn carriage rides, half-days on beaches or a visit to the 19th-century **Achilleion Palace** in the village of Gastoúri.

Zákynthos (Zante)

One of the main islands of the Ionian group, **Zákynthos** is famous for its natural springs and wildflowers, which form a contrast to the more barren landscapes of other islands. The beautiful beaches, high cliffs and fragrant banks of wildflowers have inspired many writers and poets, from Homer to Byron to Dionysios Solomos, who wrote the Greek national anthem.

Icon, Zákynthos Museum

Zákynthos Town, the principal port, is a typical Greek scene of dazzling white houses, yachts, fishing boats and tavernas. The whole town had to be rebuilt after a devastating earthquake in 1953, so there are few old buildings, but the reconstruction has been sympathetically done. Most cruise ships have to tender passengers into the port.

The focal point away from the port area is **Platía Solomoú**, on which you'll find the **Museum of Post-Byzantine Art** (open Tues–Sun 8.30am–2.30pm; admission fee). Nearby is the **Museum of Dionysios Solomos** (open daily 9am–2pm; admission fee), dedicated to the life and work of Solomos, the father of modern Greek literature, and to other prominent local people, with many portraits, clothes, furniture, icons and

Navágio beach

manuscripts to look at. Shop in the town for local wine, honey, jewellery, leather and pottery.

To appreciate the natural beauty of Zákynthos, you need to hire a bike or scooter, jump on a local bus or, best of all, walk to nearby lovely beaches and pretty villages inland. One of the most-photographed sites on the island is **Navágio beach** (Smugglers' Cove, accessible only by boat), with dramatic cliffs and a half-submerged shipwreck resting in the sand.

Kefaloniá

Kefaloniá (Cephalonia) is the largest of the Ionian islands but has a population of only 30,000 spread throughout its towns and resorts, with relatively few people living in the mountainous interior. Pine-clad Mt Énos, at 1,628m (5,340ft), in the south of Kefaloniá, is the island's highest mountain.

There are some lovely sandy beaches near the west-coast port of **Argostóli** and also along the south coast but the main towns had to be rebuilt after being badly damaged in an earthquake that hit the island in 1953. So, although Sámi and Argostóli have pretty settings, they are not as attractive as some of the better-preserved towns on other Greek islands. The real bonus of Kefaloniá, however, is that it is far less touristy than many other Greek ports of call and gives visitors a chance to experience the flavour of an authentic Greek island community.

Cruise ships call at **Sámi**, a port on the eastern side of the island. The town is set in a pretty harbour overlooked by steep wooded hills and opposite the neighbouring island of Itháki (Ithaca) 2km (1 mile) away, so it is worth being out on deck as your ship approaches harbour. Some ships dock while other (larger) ones will anchor off and tender passengers in. Either way – as with most Greek island ports – you are deposited right in the heart of town and there is certainly nothing as elaborate as a cruise terminal to pass through on your way there.

There is not much to see in Sámi itself – although it is always pleasant to pause for a drink in one of the harbour-

Captain Corelli's Mandolin

This novel, by the British author Louis de Bernières and set in Kefaloniá during World War II, was first published in 1994 and became a bestseller through word of mouth. The book concerns the exploits of Antonio Corelli, a mandolin-playing captain in the occupying Italian army, and Pelagia, daughter of the local doctor. The core of the text is a love story, but this is also set against the German invasion of 1943, after the capitulation of the Italians, and the subsequent massacre of Italian troops, and any islander found helping them, by the German army. Add in the Greek communist resistance, a ridiculous upper-class English intelligence officer who can only speak ancient Greek, and a film tie-in starring Nicolas Cage and Penélope Cruz, shot on location on Kefaloniá, and you have the Captain Corelli phenomenon.

Looking down into the Melissáni cave lake, Kefalloniá

front tavernas and to browse for arts and crafts, ceramics and
other souvenirs – but there are a couple of interesting caves
to visit in the area. The closest and most interesting are
Drongaráti, with oddly shaped stalactites and stalagmites;
and **Melissáni**, on the road to Aghía Evfimía. The sun shin-
ing down through a hole in the cave's roof onto an underground lake creates a spectacular lighting effect.

Kythira

Kýthira is the southern sister of the Ionian Islands. Emigra-
tion has taken much of the population away, so many villages are empty, or almost empty. Most ships dock at the
new port of **Diakófti**.

The island's abandoned medieval capital, reminiscient of
Mystrás, is near **Potamós**, the largest village. Most visitors
head for **Kapsáli**, a lovely double-bay port in the south. Also
of interest is **Mylopótamos**, a beautiful medieval village.

The Cyclades

For many people the Cyclades *are* Greece; other island chains are mere distractions from this blue Aegean essence. They were inhabited by 6000BC; by the third millennium a fascinating island culture flourished here, with fine arts and crafts and lively commerce. Of the 56 islands, 24 are inhabited. Mýkonos and Santoríni are popular cruise destinations.

Mýkonos

The island has had a reputation for exciting nightlife since the 1960s, which is why some ships stay late in the evening, and the streets are lined with tantalising shops and restaurants.

Pétros, mascot of Mýkonos

Outside the town the island does not have too much to offer, apart from excellent beaches on the south coast, but it is superbly located for an excursion to the neighbouring island of Delos.

Ships either dock or anchor off and use tenders. The length of stay varies from a half day to a full day with a late-evening departure.

As your ship approaches **Mýkonos Town** on the west coast, and the stark white houses and line of (now redundant) windmills come into view, this is everyone's dream of a Greek island. Cruise ships dock at Toúrlos to the east of the north-facing harbour. There is a small terminal and a shuttle bus (normally free) to take passengers to the edge of town.

From the shuttle bus drop-off, it is a short walk along the harbour to the main square, **Platía M. Mavrogénous**. The town's maze of streets and lanes can be confusing, but this is a compact, easily walkable place. As well as the trendy cafés and restaurants and glitzy shops, it also has a range of muse-

Traditional Cycladic architecture, Mýkonos

ums, including the **Folklore Museum** (open Mon–Sat 4–8pm, Sun 5–8pm; free), and **Archaeological Museum** (open Tues–Sun 8.30am–3pm; admission fee).

Delos

Most cruise lines operate tours from Mýkonos to the island of Delos, although it's quite easy to get there independently – ferries depart from the tender pier in the main town harbour. Be warned: even in good weather, the 8km (5-mile) journey can be rough. An abundance of Graeco-Roman ruins makes this island one of the most important historical and archaeological sites in Greece. The mythological birthplace of Apollo and Artemis, this tiny island was for nearly a thousand years the political and religious centre of the Aegean. Highlights include the **Sanctuary of Apollo** with its temples dedicated to Apollo and Artemis, the **Sanctuary of Dionysos**, and the stunning Lion Terrace. The artisans' houses, close to the port, are fascinating, separated by narrow lanes lined by 2,000-year-old drains, with niches for oil-burning streetlamps. The main road leads to the theatre, with superb views from the uppermost of its 43 rows.

Santoríni

Sitting in the sparkling bay created more than 3,500 years ago by a cataclysmic eruption of the Thera volcano, **Santoríni** was discovered by the Venetians in the 13th century, and named after their patron saint, Irene. Only 7,000 people live on the island, but there are a million visitors a year, most of them arriving by cruise ship and heading first for the capital, Firá, perched on the top of the 300m (1,000ft) cliffs overlooking the bay. The most interesting part of the island, however, is further south, at Akrotíri. The ancient city here was destroyed by the Thera eruption, which covered it in a sea of lava; excavations have revealed some of the original buildings.

Windmill on Santoríni

When you cruise into the bay of Santoríni, with its dramatic views of precipitous rocky cliffs, keep in mind that you are sailing into the huge crater of a still-active volcano. Sailing out of the bay at sunset is an even more impressive experience. The usual stay in port is a full day.

Ships anchor in the bay and send passengers ashore by tenders, which dock immediately below Firá. As soon as you set foot on land, you will be encouraged to pay locals for a ride up a steep flight of steps to the town on mule-back. This used to be the only alternative to walking, but then a cable car was built. This is the best option, although it can involve some queuing and the clifftop station is further from the centre of town than the top of the steps. Walking or mule-riding on your way back to the ship can be fun.

Originally founded in the 18th century, **Firá** was completely rebuilt after another, smaller volcanic eruption in 1956 and, with its whitewashed houses, shops and churches, is prettier from a distance than close-up.

A blue-domed church with extraordinary views

The main road in and out is clogged with traffic, but in the centre there are some interesting cobbled alleyways and a small museum (near the cable-car station) to explore, along with the main shopping centre (Gold Street). This runs parallel to the clifftop and is a short walk to the right of the steps and a slightly longer one to the right of the cable-car station. The views from some of the cafés down to the bay are worth the trip. The town is completely walkable.

Typical excursions include the Minoan city of **Akrotiri**, dating from before 2000BC. It was buried under metres of ash during an eruption of around 1500BC and, since 1967, the site has been painstakingly escavated to give a picture of daily life before the eruption. It is still an active dig.

Other excursions include the picturesque village of **Ía** (pronounced 'ee-a'), set on the northern cliffs and with typical Cyclades architecture, some built into the steep hillsides, and the tiny island of **Paleá Kaméni** and its hot mud baths.

Páros

⚓ **Páros** is one of the Cyclades islands that is slightly overshadowed by its more glamorous and dramatic neighbours – Mýkonos and Santoríni. The island is nonetheless very pretty, with attractive villages and many examples of traditional Cyclades 'sugar cube' architecture, set against a glorious blue sea.

First impressions are of a busy, bustling port, with ferries, fishing boats, water taxis and yachts coming and going, and a harbourfront lined with bars, cafés and tavernas.

In summer, **Parikía**, the capital, bustles with holidaymakers spilling off the ferries and enjoying the busy nightlife after dark. Inland from the waterfront, you'll find a lively market, a good place to shop for local honey, wine and olives. There's also the remains of a Venetian castle and a handsome Byzantine church, the **Ekatondapylianí**, one of the largest in the Greek islands, known as the Church of a Hundred Doors. Legend says that 99 doors have been discovered and when the hundredth is found, Constantinople will be reunited with Greece.

If you wish to travel further afield, take the hourly bus or hire a car and drive to **Náousa** in the north, a resort with good beaches and great windsurfing. Inland, **Lévkes** is a pretty medieval village of narrow streets and well-preserved buildings. Also visit **Petaloúdes**, the Valley of the Butterflies (in reality, tiger moths, at their most dazzling in June) and the Maráthi quarries, from which high-quality white marble has been taken for centuries – it was used for the famous Venus de Milo statue.

A fisherman checks his nets in Náousa harbour, Páros

Octopus drying in the sun – a familiar scene in the Cyclades

Náxos

The island of **Náxos**, the largest of the Cyclades, is closely associated with Ariadne, the daughter of King Minos of Crete who helped Theseus escape from the labyrinth and his encounter with the minotaur. Theseus took Ariadne with him from Crete but abandoned her on Náxos, where Dionysos, the god of wine and the theatre, found her and married her. The small island where they met is just to the north of the harbour capital, **Hóra**, and is now joined to the main island by a narrow spit of land. On top of the small island are the remains of a 6th-century BC Ionic **Temple of Apollo**, with its huge portal, now the island's symbol, still standing.

Hóra's thriving harbourfront has shops, restaurants and banks, but the hill behind retains the old medieval streets with arched passageways leading up to the 13th-century **castle** that was built by the Venetian Marco Sanudo. The building in which the archaeological museum is housed used to be the French School, founded in 1627 to provide schooling free of charge to both Catholic and Greek Orthodox students; these included, late in the 19th century, the writer Nikos Kazantzakis.

Crete

Crete (Kríti) is by far the largest Greek island, being 256km (159 miles) long and between 11 and 56km (7 and 35 miles) wide. A massive mountainous backbone dominates, with peaks stretching skywards to over 2,400m (7,874ft). Crete is sometimes called Megalónissos, or 'Great Island'. The capital, Iráklio, is a popular cruise destination and a handy base from which to visit the island's main tourist attraction: Knossos, of Minatour fame.

> **Crete was the cradle of European civilisation, and the Minoans – a people believed to be mythical until evidence of their existence was confirmed in the early 20th century – travelled far and wide across the eastern Mediterranean for trade. A prodigious collection of artefacts now in museums across the island shows them to be the first true Europeans, whose lives were graced by art, sports and the pursuit of pleasure.**

Iráklio

Iráklio (Heráklion) has been the capital of Crete since 1971 and is home to almost a third of the island's population. Ships usually spend enough time in Iráklio to allow for excursions to Knossos. Taxis are available at the port or, if you want to walk, you can reach the city's main square, Platía Venizélou, by turning right outside the port gates, walking along the waterfront, then turning left down 25 Avgoústou.

Arriving in **Platía Venizélou**, you'll be rewarded by the sight of the lovely, 17th-century Morosini Fountain with its famous lion sculptures. You also find yourself at the heart of

Iráklio's shopping district, a good area to hunt for local ceramics, lace and sculptures.

Before you leave Platía Venizélou, have a look at the 13th-century, Venetian-built basilica, **Ágios Márkos**, which is now an eyecatching art gallery; a little way north is a beautifully restored 17th-century Venetian *loggia*. Just to the south, a museum housed in the church of **Aghía Ekateríni** (open Mon–Fri 9.30am–2.30pm; admission fee) contains some beautiful icons. High on your list of things to see should be the **Archaeological Museum** (open Mon 12–5pm, Tues– Sun 8am–5pm; admission fee), to the north of the other major square, Platía

Boats at harbour in Iráklio

Elevtherías, which is one of the best in Greece. The tourist office is almost next door.

If you are still intrigued by Crete's history, take a look at Iráklio's city walls, which were constructed by the Venetians in the second half of the 15th century. Here you'll find the tomb of Iráklio-born Nikos Kazantzakis, author of *Zorba the Greek*. There's another Italian fortress, the 16th-century **Rocca al Mare**, in the old harbour.

Excursions from Iráklio

All cruise lines offer excursions to the extensive Minoan remains of the **Palace of Knossos** (open daily 8am–7pm;

admission fee), 5km (3 miles) from Iráklio. According to legend, the palace was the labyrinth of King Minos, where he imprisoned the minotaur.

This huge site, covering over 2 hectares (about 5½ acres), is stunning and mysterious, despite the often large crowds. Much of what you see was reconstructed by the British archaeologist Sir Arthur Evans, who excavated the site in the early 1900s, and his work is controversial. Nonetheless, the palace complex – grand stairway, throne room, royal apartments, dolphin wall painting, giant storage jars – is impressive indeed. Another popular excursion is 'Scenic Crete' to various other historic sites.

The Dodecanese

The Dodecanese islands take their name from the Greek phrase *dódeka nísi*, meaning 12 islands, although there are far more than a dozen in its number. Until 1912 they were part of the Ottoman Empire, from 1912 to 1947 they were ruled by Italy and in 1947 they were passed into Greek hands. The main islands exhibit faded remains of a Muslim influence, though this was just one of several cultures to leave its mark.

Kós

Birthplace of Hippocrates, the father of modern medicine, **Kós** has always been known for the Asklepion, its sanctuary and ancient medical school. Nowadays, the island is a popular holiday resort, with beautiful beaches, packed in summer, and a partly wooded interior. There are several resorts, some sadly encapsulating the worst of modern package tourism.

In **Kós Town**, where ships dock, Italian-style architecture blends with the Turkish quarter's minarets. Look for the old castle on the starboard side as you approach. The town centre, where narrow, mainly pedestrianised, streets are lined with shops and tavernas, is not far from the dock. If you're here overnight, go ashore in the evening, as there's a lively buzz and shops are open late.

Sights include a Roman *agora*, a restored Roman villa, and an 18th-

Fresco of Minoan women, Knossos

century mosque. There's also the splendid collection of the **Archaeological Museum** (open Tues–Sun 8.30am–3pm; admission fee), near the municipal market.

The **Asklepion** (open Tues–Sun 8.30am–3pm; admission fee), on an elevated site 4km (2½ miles) southwest of town, has stunning sea views. It was a medical school for nearly 1,000 years, although it may not have been founded until shortly after the death of Hippocrates (c.460–370BC).

Pátmos

⚓ The main attraction of **Pátmos** is the impressive **Monastery of St John the Theologian** (open daily 8.30am–1pm, also 4–6pm Sun, Tues, Thur; free), begun in 1088, and the **Monastery of the Apocalypse** (open daily 8am–1pm; free), begun in 1090 and containing the Grotto of the Apocalypse, both above the harbour town of Skála. **Hóra**, the main town, has many early 19th-century houses. Pátmos also has many well-protected bays and fine beaches: Mellí, Agriolívadho, Kámbos, Vágia, Livádi Geranoú and Kakóskala all on the east coast north of Skála; Lámbi on the north coast; and Psilí Ámmos on the east coast south of Skála.

Rhodes

⚓ **Rhodes** (Ródos) is the top tourism destination in the Dodecanese, largely because of its magnificent, walled, medieval Old Town – one of the largest in Europe. It's full of package tourists and the inevitable tat shops and fast-food joints that follow in their wake, but there's fine architecture and narrow cobbled streets to explore, and plenty of picturesque, terraced restaurants dotted about. Ships usually spend more than half a day here to allow for trips to Líndos.

Large ships go into the Commercial Port to the east of the Old Town; smaller vessels and tenders can get into Mandráki Harbour, which dates back to medieval times. Rhodes is easily walkable, and the Old Town (the bit worth seeing) is a 20-minute walk from the port.

Divided into three quarters – the Knights, the Turkish and the Jewish – Rhodes Old Town charts the island's entire history within its sturdy walls. Enter via St Catherine's Gate and head right to see the magnificent fountain in **Platía Evréon Martýron**, which features bronze sea horses.

The famous 14th-century **Street of the Knights** is a must for lovers of the Gothic order, which predominates here. The Inns of the various (eight) 'tongues' spoken by the Knights stand in a row, with arched doorways and emblems carved above them. The road is a medieval thoroughfare which houses the 14th-century **Palace of the Grand Masters** (open Mon 12.30–3pm, Tues–Sun 8.30am–3pm; admission fee), which should be your next stop. Though partially destroyed by a gunpowder explosion in 1856, it was reconstructed in grand style by the Italians (Mussolini planned to use it as a holiday home to suit his sense of grandeur). Now a museum, it contains antique furniture, sculptures and mosaics.

Street of the Knights

In this area you'll also find the 14th-century **Hospital of the Knights of St John**, which now houses the archaeological museum (open Tues–Sun 8.30am–3pm; admission fee). Nearby

Líndos, a popular excursion from Rhodes Town

is the **Museum of Decorative Arts** (open Tues–Sun 8.30am–3pm; admission fee) which is well worth a look, and the pink-domed, 16th-century **Mosque of Suleyman** and the **Byzantine Museum**, housed in an 11th-century church.

Excursions from Rhodes Town

Many people take a tour to **Líndos**, 44km (27 miles) to the south. Its strong acropolis supports a scaffolded Hellenistic Athena temple and another Knights' castle. Clustered below in the village are imposing mansions built by local sea-captains. Italian, German and British bohemians first rediscovered Líndos in the 1960s, but its role as an artists' colony has long since been replaced by one as a package-tour dormitory; midsummer visits are not recommended, when the narrow, cobbled streets are crowded.

Another excursion is to the site of ancient **Kamiros**, 36km (22 miles) south of Rhodes Town on the west coast.

The Northeast Aegean

Many of the rugged islands in the northern Aegean lie closer to Turkey than Greece. Remote Lésvos is the largest, a fertile, olive-growing island; the other one featured here, Híos, was devasted by an 1811 earthquake but still has medieval features.

Híos (Chios)

Híos, a craggy island in the eastern Aegean, near the Turkish coast, is said to be the birthplace of Homer. Ships dock or tender at **Híos Town** (also called Hóra), on the east coast. The harbour is busy, with tavernas, shops and cafés, as is what's left of the old quarter of the citadel after an earthquake destroyed the city in 1881. Buses run to beautiful beaches nearby. Further afield, the Byzantine mosaics at **Néa Moní Monastery** are famous, while the exteriors of the houses in the village of **Pyrgí** are decorated with striking black and white geometrical patterns in a style called *xystá*.

Lésvos (Lesbos)

Just 10km (6 miles) off the Turkish coast, **Lésvos** (Lésbos) is best known for its olive oil, and its rolling hills are dense with olive groves and pine forests. This island has a colourful history and ruins dating back to 3000BC have been found. It is thought to be the birthplace of the poet Sappho and attracts many gay women in summer. The capital, **Mytilíni** (sometimes, confusingly, used for the whole island), has neoclassical mansions, antiques shops and a folk art museum.

Lésvos is famous for its olive trees

The Sporádes

This group comprises four 'scattered islands' (Sporádes): Skiáthos, Skópelos, Alónisos and Skýros.

⚓ The most heavily developed of these islands (although still beautiful), is **Skiáthos**. It has one town; a famous 19th-century author, Papadiamantis; two preserved monasteries, including the beautiful 18th-century Evangelistrías Monastery; and 62 beaches, some of the best in Greece.

⚓ **Skópelos** is less developed than Skiáthos, and its two seaside towns, Skiáthos and Glóssa, both mostly of traditional white architecture, are prettier. Of the main beaches of Stávylos, Agnóntas, Limnonári, Pánormos and Miliá, Pánormos is the most commercialised. After the island's main town, Hóra, was damaged by an earthquake in 1965, the residents moved to where the boats land, Patitíri, a concrete collection of buildings putting on its best face with potted plants and vines. The Monk Seal Protection Society is based in Stení Vála, and the northern Sporades are a marine wildlife reserve to protect the small remaining population of these creatures in the Mediterranean. The best beaches near Patitíri are Rousoúm Gialós, Kokkinnókastro, Levtós Gialós, Miliá, Hryssí Miliá and Vótsi.

Typically peaceful Sporádes cove

The south of **Skýros** is ⚓ barren and windswept, while its northern section is wooded and green. The white buildings of Skýros Town rising up the mountain are beautiful, and the village streets, negotiable only on foot, are quite pleasant. Tourism is active along the main street running between the rarely used village square and an idealised statue of

The Church of Christ is a prominent landmark on Skópelos

the English poet Rupert Brooke, who died here in 1915, but neither the town nor the island ever gets overly crowded.

The Argo-Saronic Gulf Islands

Cruise ships occasionally call at the islands of Aegina (Égina), Póros and Ýdra (Hydra), located in the Saronic Gulf close to Athens *(see page 158)*. These islands, popular with Athenians for a weekend break, will also give you a good taste of island life before or after a cruise, as they're easily accessible from the capital's port, Piraeus, by ferry.

Aegina is mountainous, with vines, olives, figs, almonds ⚓ and pistachios its main industries, alongside tourism and sponge fishing. **Ýdra**, in contrast, is barren and rocky, with ⚓ donkeys used for transport instead of cars, and massive underground cisterns where water was once stored. **Póros**, a speck ⚓ off the northeast coast of the Peloponnese, is greener, with a pretty principal town clinging to a hillside, topped by a church.

Turkey

Climate The Marmara zone has a typically Mediterranean climate with hot summers and mild winters, with temperatures rising the further south you go.

Time Zone GMT+2 hours; GMT+3 hours in summer.

Opening Times Most shops are closed on Sunday, but major stores open all week. The large shopping centres and smart clothes shops open later, at 10am, closing between 8pm and 10pm. Small neighbourhood stores are generally open 8am–8.30/9pm. Banks are open Monday–Friday 8.30am–12pm, 1.30–5pm; a few main branches also open Saturday morning.

What to Buy Textiles, clothing, carpets, pottery, metalwork, semi-precious and precious stones and jewellery, leather and glass.

Money Matters Turkish lira (TL), which has one of the lowest unit values of any currency in the world.

Festivals and Public Holidays 1 January, 23 April, 19 May, 30 August, 29 October, 10 November.

Etiquette Beachwear is worn only on the beach, and topless sunbathing is frowned on. Non-Muslims should not enter a mosque during prayer time, and not at all on Friday, the holy day. Both men and women should be modestly dressed: for women a longish skirt or trousers and covered shoulders; for men, shorts are not acceptable. Before entering remove your shoes. Women may be asked to cover their heads, so carry a scarf or hat.

Tipping It is customary to tip a small amount to anyone who does you a small service – the equivalent of about 20–70 pence/US30c–$1. In restaurants, round the bill up by 10–15 percent; if service has been included, leave 5 percent in cash for the waiter. Taxis are the exception: you don't tip taxi drivers and they do not expect it, though you can round the fare up .

Hazards and Security Diarrhoea is the main hazard. Drink only bottled water and ensure that cooked food is piping hot. It's safest to eat freshly prepared local produce. Other major hazards in summer include heatstroke and sunburn.

Emergency Telephone Numbers Police 155; ambulance 112; fire 110.

Istanbul's Süleymaniye at sunset

TURKEY

The eastern Mediterranean is where East meets West, where the everyday seems exotic. It is also an area of great variety and a fusion of several cultures. The city of Istanbul, once Constantinople and the power centre of the sprawling Ottoman Empire, is a glittering delight; and the port of Canakkale draws visitors interested in the memorials and cemeteries of the Gallipoli Peninsula, where so many died in World War I. Further south, Kuşadası is the access port for the ancient city of Ephesus, while Bodrum and Marmaris are busy tourist resorts.

Istanbul

Be up on deck as your ship approaches **Istanbul**; its glittering domes and minarets make the skyline of this ancient city one of the world's most memorable sights. Some 3,000 years old, spanning two continents and a crucible of cultures,

Lokum (Turkish Delight) at the Spice Bazaar in Istanbul

Istanbul is not really a city to see in a rush, so if your cruise begins or ends here, it's well worth tagging on a few days' stay ashore. However, you can see the main sights on a two-day cruise call so, assuming you have only that much time, this chapter covers the experiences and attractions you really shouldn't miss.

First, get your bearings; the Bosphorus Strait, which links the Black Sea with the Sea of Marmara, cuts through Istanbul, dividing the European sector from the Asian sector in the East. Your ship will arrive in European Istanbul (ships dock at Karaköy, at the northern end of the Galata Bridge), which is further divided by an estuary known as the Golden Horn.

Eminönü

Istanbul's main tourist attractions are concentrated in the Sultanahmet district, the heart of the Old City. En route, pass through the Eminönü district (also the terminus for the tram and ferries), directly south of the Galata Bridge. The wide square south of the bridge is dominated by the **New Mosque** (Yeni Camii). Commissioned in 1597, it was not completed until 1663, making the Yeni Camii the youngest of Istanbul's classical mosques.

The large archway to the right of the mosque is the entrance to the **Spice Bazaar**, also known as the Egyptian Bazaar (Mısır Çarşısı). It was opened a few years before the Yeni Camii, and its revenues originally paid for repairs to the mosque complex. Inside, the air is heady with the mingled aromas of ginger, pepper, cinnamon, cloves and freshly ground coffee.

The Old City

The Old City is home to Istanbul's most magnificent mosques, palaces and churches, as well as the vibrant Grand Bazaar. Trams run to the Old City from Eminönü.

Of the few remains of the Byzantine city, the most remarkable building is the **Aya Sofya** (open Tues–Sun 9.30am–4.30pm, Jun–Oct 9am–7pm; admission fee). For nearly 1,000 years this was the greatest church in Christendom, an architectural wonder built by the Byzantine Empire to impress the world. The last Christian service held in Haghia Sophia took place on 28 May 1453, the day before Constantinople finally fell to the Turks. Mehmet the Conqueror immediately converted the building to a mosque, and built a brick minaret at the southeast corner. Haghia Sophia served as a mosque until 1935, when it became a museum.

> It's also worthwhile crossing the Galata Bridge to the New City (Beyoğlu), where attractions include the famous Janissary Band, which performs at the Military Museum daily at 3–4pm.

Northwest of Haghia Sophia is the walled enclosure of **Topkapı Palace** (open Wed–Mon 9.30am–5pm, June–Oct 9am–7pm; admission fee), the former residence and seat of government of the Ottoman sultans. Begun in 1462 by Mehmet the Conqueror, it was extended by each succeeding sultan until it became a miniature city, containing mosques, libraries, stables, kitchens, schools, the imperial mint, treasuries, barracks, armouries, government offices and audience halls. At its height it had a population of nearly 4,000.

Sultan Abdül Mecit moved into the newly built Dolmabahçe Palace in 1853, and by 1909 Topkapı was abandoned. In 1924 it was converted into a museum, and has been undergoing a programme of restoration ever since. If pushed for time, highlights are, in order of importance, the Harem (the private quarters of the sultan, his mother and his wives and concubines; open 10am–4pm, 30-minute guided tour only), the Treasury and the Pavilion of the Holy Mantle.

From Topkapı's First Court, a narrow cobbled lane leads to the Fifth Court, which contains three excellent museums (open Tues–Sat 9am–7pm; single admission fee for all three). The **Archaeological Museum** (Arkeoloji Müzesi) has been expanded to include galleries devoted to Cyprus, Syria and Palestine, the Phrygians, Troy and Anatolia, from the Palaeolithic to the Iron Age. Its main attraction is the magnificent collection of sarcophagi, especially the Alexander Sarcophagus, decorated with scenes of hunting and battle.

The long, narrow stretch of parkland that runs southwest from Haghia Sophia is known as the **Hippodrome** (At Meydanı). It occupies the area covered by a stadium built in AD203 by Emperor Septimus Severus for chariot-racing and other public events and later enlarged by Constantine the Great. It could hold an audience of 100,000.

Dominating the skyline of the Hippodrome are the six minarets of the **Blue Mosque**. Known in Turkish as the *Sultan*

Ahmet Camii (Mosque of Sultan Ahmet), it was built between 1609 and 1616 for the Sultan Ahmet I, after which it became the city's principal imperial mosque because of its proximity to the sultan's palace at Topkapı. To savour the full effect of the architect's skill, enter the courtyard through the gate which opens onto the Hippodrome.

From the Blue Mosque, follow the tram tracks on Divan Yolu west to the bustling **Grand Bazaar**. The Kapalı Çarşı (Covered Market) of Istanbul is the world's largest covered bazaar, with about 4,000 shops, as well as banks, cafés, restaurants, mosques and a post office, crammed together in a grid of 66 narrow streets that total 8km (5 miles) in length. Mehmet the Conqueror built the first covered market on this site in 1461. It has been rebuilt several times after destruction by fire and earthquake, most recently in 1954 and again, to a lesser degree, in 1974. It is fairly easy to find your way, as most of the streets follow a pattern and are signposted.

The Grand Bazaar

If time allows, take a tram to **Beyazıt**, site of Istanbul University and the **Süleymaniye** (Mosque of Süleyman the Magnificent). Seen as the finest Ottoman building in Istanbul, the mosque is a tribute to the Ottoman Empire's 'Golden Age'.

For an excellent overview of Istanbul take a boat trip up the Bosphorus (two sailings

Sailing the Bosphorus

a day, at 10.35am and 1.35pm) from the pier at Eminönü *(see page 194)*. The ferry weaves back and forth between Europe and Asia, calling first at Befliktafl and then at a string of attractive villages. You can remain on the boat for the round trip, or disembark anywhere and simply return by bus or taxi.

Kusadası (Ephesus)

Kuşadası may not be the traditional fishing village of yesteryear, but despite commercialism there are still pockets of old-world Turkey, notably in the atmospheric narrow streets of the Kaleici quarter, the oldest part of town, and good beaches nearby. Kuşadası's proximity to the ancient city of **Ephesus** means it attracts ships for full-day stays to allow for excursions. Beyond the modern ferry port, a 350-m (1,050-ft) causeway connects Kuşadası to **Güvercin Adası** (Pigeon Island), which is topped by a 13th-century Byzantine castle and ringed with gardens and cafés.

Ephesus

Some 17km (10½ miles) inland from Kuşadası, **Ephesus** (Efes) is one of the best-preserved of Turkey's ancient cities. Its marble streets and monuments have been extensively excavated and restored by archaeologists, and with only a little imagination it is easy to transport yourself to Roman times.

Ionian Greeks from the island of Samos settled in Ephesus c.1000BC. The site was associated with the worship of the

Anatolian mother-goddess Cybele, who became merged with the Greek Artemis. The Temple of Artemis, one of the Seven Wonders of the World, was erected in her honour. The city was ruled in turn by the Lydians, the Persians and the Attalid kings of Pergamon until 133BC, when Attalus III bequeathed his kingdom, and Ephesus with it, to the Romans. Ephesus was one of the most important cities in the new province of Asia, with a population of 200,000, and grew wealthy on the proceeds of trade. But its greatness was linked to its fine natural harbour, and when this silted up in the 3rd century AD, the city went into decline. The site was rediscovered by the British archaeologist J.T. Wood in 1869 after six years of searching. Many of the ruins visible today date from the Roman period, between the 1st century BC and 2nd century AD.

Most of the guided tours commence at the **Magnesian Gate** and head downhill along the main street. The first

The Library of Celcus at Ephesus

buildings inside the gate are the **Odeum** (council chamber) and **Prytaneum**, where archaeologists discovered two important statues of Artemis. The marble-paved **Street of the Curetes** leads through the Gate of Hercules to the remarkable **Temple of Hadrian**, with an arched doorway capped by the head of Tyche, goddess of fortune. At the corner of Marble Street, on the right, are the **Baths of Scholastica**, which also included a brothel.

Rising up ahead is the imposing façade of the **Library of Celsus**, built in AD110 by a Roman consul as a memorial to his father, and restored in the 1970s. Marble Street leads from the library to the **Great Theatre**, which provided seating for 25,000 people, and still accommodates the crowds who gather for shows during the annual Ephesus International Festival.

Bodrum

⚓ **Bodrum**, which is built on the ruins of ancient Halicarnassus and is the birthplace of the historian Herodotus, combines fascinating history and scenic beauty with some of tourism's worst excesses. It's undeniably pretty but hugely crowded at the peak of summer. The approach to the harbour, however, is stunning, with the crusader castle of St Peter dominating a small promontory and polished wooden *gulets* (sailing boats) gliding in and out of the port. Cruise passengers are tendered in from their ships but, once in, all Bodrum's attractions are within easy walking distance.

The tomb of the former ruler, Mausolus, is considered one of the Seven Wonders of the Ancient World and gave rise to the word mausoleum. Only the foundations remain. The castle of St Peter, now the **Museum of Underwater Archaeology** (open Tues–Sun 9am–12pm, 2–7pm; admission fee), houses treasures including the hull of a Byzantine ship.

Behind the harbour, extending towards the castle, are narrow streets dotted with shops, nightclubs and rooftop bars. By night, these streets are packed with revellers and clubbers, but the harbourside restaurants are a pleasant way to spend an evening ashore. Bodrum has no beaches to speak of; you need to take a *dolmus* (shared taxi) further along the peninsula for sunbathing and swimming.

Marmaris

Marmaris is one of the most popular holiday resorts in Turkey, and has consequently suffered from over-development. Nonetheless its setting is stunning – on a vast bay ringed with mountains and pine forests, the water often brilliant with the

Gulets in Bodrum harbour

white sails of thousands of yachts in summer. Cruise ships either tender or dock at the ferry terminal, from which a small square leads to the narrow streets and bazaar of the Old Town. This has spread out around a small citadel, dating from 3000BC and subsequently rebuilt by Alexander the Great and Suleyman the Magnificent. There are numerous tavernas overlooking the seafront – those situated higher up towards the Citadel are least touristy.

If you have a whole day to spare, take a boat trip to the exquisite **Cleopatra's Island**, a 12-km (8-mile) minibus ride and short boat trip from the town (bookable through a local operator at the port). It's famous for its clear water and powdery white sand.

Cyprus

Climate Cyprus has a long, hot and dry summer with relatively low humidity; a short spring and autumn; and a mild, wet winter.

Time Zone GMT+2 hours.

Opening Times Shops are open on Monday, Tuesday, Thursday and Friday until 6pm in winter, 7.30pm in summer, Wednesday and Saturday until 2pm in winter and summer. Closing times may be earlier in spring and autumn (about 7pm) and most shops shut for the afternoon siesta some time between 1 and 4pm in summer.

What to Buy Aside from the local wine, spirits and halloumi cheese, souvenirs include various handicrafts such as lace, leather goods, pottery, jewellery, silk products, glassware, woodcarvings and embroidery.

Money Matters The unit of currency in the Republic of Cyprus is the Cyprus pound (CY£), called the lira in Greek.

Festivals and Public Holidays 1, 6 January, 25 March, 1 April, 1 May, 15 August, 1 October, 28 October, 24, 25, 26 December.

Etiquette When you visit a monastery take care to be appropriately attired. People wearing shorts, no shirts, backless tops, short dresses and swimwear are not admitted (sometimes even women in trousers). Shoes should be removed before entering a mosque. Bartering is not really a feature of shopping in Cyprus.

Tipping A 10 percent service charge is levied in hotels and restaurants so a tip is not obligatory, although small change is always welcomed. If service is not included, a 10 percent tip is standard in restaurants. It is traditional to give taxi drivers 10 percent extra, and porters, tour guides, hairdressers and cloakroom attendants 50 cents to CY£1.

Hazards and Security Cyprus is one of the safest places to visit in the Mediterranean. Crime is low and people are generally relaxed and hospitable.

Drugs and Medicines In all cities there are hospitals with English-speaking doctors.

Emergency Telephone Numbers Police 112; ambulance 112; fire 112.

Cypriot fisherman at harbour

CYPRUS

The third-largest island in the Mediterranean, Cyprus became an independent republic in 1960; after the 1974 Turkish invasion, however, it became divided between the Turkish north and Greek south. The Greek section (roughly two-thirds of the island) dominates the tourist scene, with the popular resorts of Agía Napa – famous for its non-stop nightlife – and Páfos in the southwest.

Much of the island remains unspoilt by hotel or resort developments, with plenty of rugged coastline and mountain scenery left to explore and enjoy. There are nearly 200km (120 miles) of hiking trails, and notable archaeological sites, particularly in and around Páfos, one of several UNESCO World Cultural Heritage sites on the island. Both can be reached from the cruise ports of Larnaca and Limassol; although Páfos is a long way west (70km/43 miles from Limassol), fast roads make the journey easy.

Limassol

The second-largest town in Cyprus and the centre of the local wine industry, **Limassol** is also the island's main cruise port and a major resort in its own right. Ships always dock rather than anchor off and almost always stay a full day, although departures are normally early rather than late evening.

There is nothing too memorable about sailing into this busy port, although the Troodos Mountains do form an attractive backdrop. The local authority operates a shuttle bus for cruise visitors to take them the 3km (2 miles) into the centre of Limassol. If you prefer to walk, it's a 20- to 30-minute, rather uninspiring hike to the old port, the start of Limassol proper.

Central Limassol is walkable, either along the coast road, which has a manicured promenade overlooking its beach, or through the main shopping area (Agíou Andreou Street), which runs parallel to the coast road and is partly pedestrianised.

Colourful fishing boats in Limassol's old port

Just across from the old port is the **Crusader Castle**, where Richard the Lionheart married Berengaria. The castle later belonged to the Knights of St John of Jerusalem, then to the Turks. It now houses the fascinating **Medieval Museum** (open Mon–Sat 9am–5pm, Sun 10am–1pm; admission fee). Close by is the Turkish quarter, with its twin mosques and Turkish bathhouse.

View of Limassol's rooftops from the castle battlements

Off to the right, the colourful market is fun. Going north, you can visit the **Agía Trias** (Holy Trinity) church and end up in the Municipal Gardens, where there is an open-air theatre and a rather sad little zoo.

Excursions from Limassol

Situated about halfway along the south coast of Cyprus, Limassol is an ideal base for exploring the island, as none of the main towns or attractions is more than 60–90 minutes' drive away. There are hourly buses on weekdays from the marketplace in Limassol to the capital, Nicosia (Lefkosia), but services are less frequent at weekends and so are best avoided – as are the patchy bus services to Larnaca and to the hill resort of Platres. A better bet are the shared taxis that link Limassol, Larnaca, Páfos and Nicosia. They run every half-hour (hourly at weekends) and usually will pick up and drop off anywhere within those towns, but you do have to ring to book (local tourist offices have lists of numbers).

A tour of the impressive ruins of **Kourion** (open summer: daily 9am–7.30pm; winter: daily 9am–5pm; admission fee), a short distance west of Limassol, is offered by many cruise lines; alternatively take one of the public buses that leave from Limassol Castle throughout the day. Not the least of its attractions is its spectacular setting high on a bluff above Episkopi Bay.

The site is large but highlights include the reconstructed Roman theatre (AD50–175), the Roman Villa of Eustolios, an early Christian basilica, the remains of the city's ancient stadium, the Sanctuary of Apollo Hylates and the Temple of Apollo, partially reconstructed to appear as it did in AD100.

Páfos is always offered as a shore excursion: the 95-hectare (235-acre) site of the ancient city, **Nea Páfos** has some extraordinary mosaics in its excavated houses. The modern, lower town and resort of **Kato Páfos** has a pretty harbour and good fish restaurants.

Kourion's Roman theatre

Larnaca

Larnaca is not quite as well located for touring Cyprus as ⚓
Limassol, which is why many ships visiting Cyprus use the
latter. Nevertheless, it has a number of places of historical interest, and is much closer to Nicosia than Limassol.

Cruise visitors disembark just across the road from the town
centre. The harbour promenade makes a pleasant walk, past the
marina. A mixture of hotels, shops, restaurants and tavernas
line the front, and the beach is good – better than the one at
Limassol. Worth a longer walk or short taxi ride (to the west of
the harbour front) are the clifftop 17th-century **fort and
medieval museum** and the nearby **Ágios Lazarus** church.

In the town, the **Archaeological Museum** (open Mon–Sat
9am–5pm, Sun 10am–1pm; admission fee) and the collection
of prehistoric and medieval artefacts in the **Pierides Foun-
dation Museum** (open Oct–mid-Jun Mon–Fri 9am–1pm,
3–6pm, Sat 9am–1pm; mid–Jun–Sept 9am–1pm, 4–7pm; admission fee) are both worth seeing.

Nicosia

The island's capital, **Nicosia**, is an hour's drive from Larnaca.
Amid the prosperous bustle of the town's southern sector, it is
easy to forget the stretches of wall and barbed wire that mark
this place as a divided capital. The Old Town is completely surrounded by impressive 16th-century fortifications. A magnet
for visitors is the **Laïki Geitonia** (Popular Neighbourhood),
which recreates something of the atmosphere of old Nicosia.
On the eastern side of the city is the **Archbishop's Palace**,
which houses one of the finest museums on the island, the
Byzantine Museum (open Mon–Fri 9am–4.30pm, Sat
9am–1pm; admission fee), with a superb collection of icons.
The island's finest collection of antiquities is housed in the
Cyprus Museum (open Mon–Sat 9am–5pm, Sun 10am–1pm;
admission fee) on Leoforos Mouseiou, just west of the old city.

A donkey-load of freshly dyed wool

MOROCCO

Intricate medinas, mysterious desert kasbahs and endlessly fascinating souks – such is the exotic appeal of Morocco. Cruise destinations include Casablanca, Agadir and Tangier.

Casablanca

Casablanca's name betrays its European origins – founded as a trading town on the Atlantic coast of Morocco, the original Portuguese name was Casa Branca, the 'White House'. It remained a backwater until it was occupied by the French in 1907. Under the Protectorate it grew to become Morocco's busiest port, its most populous city and the economic and industrial capital of the kingdom, accounting for more than half of the country's industrial output. In Arabic, the city is called Dar el Baida – 'White House' – but most Moroccans refer to it as 'Casa'. Today the city has a population estimated at between 3 and 5 million, making it Africa's second largest, after Cairo. It bears no resemblance to its 'sin city' image in the movie of the same name that made it famous.

The heart of the modern city is around **place Mohammed V**, where all the city's thoroughfares meet. Between here and the port, the old *medina* is lined with shops. The city's main sight is the **Grand Mosque of Hassan II** (guided tours daily except Fri 9am, 10am, 11am and 2pm). Completed in 1994, it stands on recalimed land west of the port and is the largest mosque in the world outside Mecca. Unusually for a mosque, visitors can enter all the buildings, not just the courtyard. The interior is a dazzling tour de force of Arabic architectural motifs, amplified by the scale of the structure. A glass lift takes you up the side of the minaret, the tallest in the world at 210m (700m) and topped by a laser beam that points towards Mecca.

Typical excursions from Casablanca include full-day trips to Rabat and Marrakech.

Morocco

Climate Summer is long, hot and dry. Winter is short and mild.

Time Zone GMT all year round.

Opening Times These vary according to the time of year and at Ramadan. As a guide, Mon–Sat 8.30am–noon, 2.30–6.30pm. Some shops close on Friday (Muslim holy day).

Money Matters Dirham (dh), divided into 100 centimes.

Festivals and Public Holidays Religious holidays are determined by the lunar calendar, so vary each year. State holidays are fixed, at: 1, 11 January, 1 May, 14, 20, 21 August, 6, 18 November.

Etiquette Women should dress with consideration for Muslim sensibilities. Remove shoes to enter mosques and do not enter during prayers.

Tipping A couple of dirhams for small services; 10–15 percent for taxi drivers if on meter (nothing if price agreed beforehand).

Emergency Telephone Numbers Police 19; ambulance and fire 15.

Entrance to the Royal Palace in Rabat, Morocco's capital

Rabat

The capital of Morocco, **Rabat**, is based around the twin poles of its vast souk and the massive, over-powering fortress of the **Oudaia Kasbah**, now a residential quarter with the delightful Andalusian Garden in its midst, leading to the **Museum of Moroccan Arts** (open daily except Tues 9am–noon and 2.30–5.30pm).

On the eastern edge of town, the **Mausoleum of Mohammed V** (open daily 8am–6.30pm) is the burial place of the king who achieved independence for Morocco in 1965. Protected by guards in Berber warrior dress, the mausoleum is a lavish celebration of Moroccan craftsmanship.

The 2,000-year history of Rabat and Morocco is covered in Rabat's **Archaeological Museum** (open daily except Tues 9am–noon and 2.30–6pm), which is rich in finds from the prehistoric and Roman eras. Some of the museum's sculptures come from the Roman town of **Sala Colonia** (now known as the Chellah), whose ruins survive outside the walls of Rabat.

Marrakech

Founded in 1062 by Yusuf ibn Tashfin, the ancient city of **Marrakech** is situated where the Sahara meets the snow-capped Atlas Mountains. This gateway to mountain and desert is the meeting place of African, Arabic and Berber Morocco, as people from all over the region meet to trade in the bustling souks. Looking for entertainment, they drift at the end of the day to the central square, the **Djemaa el Fna** (literally 'the Assembly of the Dead', because the heads of executed criminals were once displayed here), where drummers summon up audiences for the plethora of storytellers, snake charmers, singers, fortune tellers and fire-eaters that throng here.

On one side of the square is the **Koutoubia Minaret**, one of the great monuments of the 12th-century Almohad dynasty. On the opposite side, rue Souk Smarie will take you into the city's souks – each specialising in a different commodity, be it pottery, leather or antiques.

To the south is the walled town or *medina*. Here, you will find the **Mosque al Mansour** and the entrance to the Saadian Tombs, a series of lavishly decorated 16th-century rooms where the sultans of the Saadian imperial family are buried.

Water-seller in colourful Djemaa el Fna, Marrakech

Agadir

Named after its 16th-century *agadir*, or fortress, this city was rebuilt after an earthquake in 1960, and the new city sits beside the clean golden sands of its bay. Tree-lined avenues and open squares contrast with the narrow crowded streets of more traditional Moroccan towns. Trips to both Marrakech *(see opposite)* and Taroudant *(see page 212)* are offered from here.

Taroudant

Located 25km (40 miles) from Agadir, **Taroudant** is one of Morocco's more easy-going destinations. Surrounded by olive groves, citrus orchards and green fields, all watered with the melting snows of the High Atlas, it is at the commercial hub of the Souss Valley. At a time when all coastal towns were open to naval attack, Taroudant's inland location and high walls made it the natural choice as the region's capital. Its impressive fortifications, built by the Saadians during the 16th century and in good repair, are the town's most striking attraction. Within the walls, the dusty squares and shady souks offer great shopping opportunities for carpets, leather and Berber jewellery.

Tangier

Morocco's oldest continually populated city, **Tangier** dates back to 1000BC when it was founded by the Berbers. From

Mounds of aromatic spices in the souk at Taroudant

1932, it was a playground for the wealthy, and although it was unified with Morocco in 1956, it still retains a cosmopolitan air. It offers a true flavour of old Maghreb Africa, with its

> In Morocco, as in all Muslim countries, it is the custom not to eat with your left hand – nor should you use it when greeting anyone.

hidden courtyard gardens, grand mosques and churches and bustling kasbah. In a prime position overlooking the Strait of Gibraltar, Tangier is a port of call in its own right, rather than a gateway to other Moroccan cities, though some ships stay for less than a full day. The cruise ship dock is just 800m/yds from the city centre.

The kasbah – set at the highest point of the *medina* – is a hive of activity; here you can see local craftsmen practise the traditional arts of carpet weaving, leather working and pottery making, and you can buy the finished products – after a good haggle over a glass of mint tea.

Tangier's **medina** (near the harbour) was originally built by the Romans, and its grand mosque stands on the foundations of a temple to Neptune, god of the sea, while Petit Socco Square covers what used to be the forum. The **Grand Socco** (otherwise known as Place du 9 Avril 1947) is the heart of the *medina* and crammed with traders from the mountain villages.

The kasbah has, in its time, been home to Roman governors, Byzantine nobles, Arab princes and Portuguese crusaders – as well as the British, who demolished the medieval fortress when they left Tangier in 1685. The fortress was rebuilt by Sultan Moulay Ishmael in the 17th century. For a fine example of Moroccan architecture, visit the kasbah's **Dar el Makhzen**, built in the 17th century as a home for the sultans and their harems. Nowadays it's an art museum. Another lovely building – also now an art museum – is the **former American Embassy**, off rue du Portugal near the Grand Socco.

Chechias (tasselled hats) are still handmade in the souk, Tunis

TUNISIA

The wealth of sightseeing opportunities in Tunisia belies the country's small size. Deservedly, vibrant Tunis is one of the most popular ports of call in North Africa – and the gateway to the ruined city of Carthage. The capital's pleasing blend of European and Arab culture is repeated, on a small scale, at Bizerte and Sidi-Bou-Saïd.

Tunis

⚓ **Tunis** is a city with many faces. On the one hand, it's the modern capital of the Tunisian Republic, a city of tree-lined boulevards, modern buildings and bustling pavement cafés, which has a distinctly European flavour. On the other, it has a totally different character, determined by its medieval Arab *medina* (old town), an exotic maze of narrow, angled streets lined with tiny shops, grand mosques and impressive palaces.

Tunis is usually a day's stay for cruise ships. Approaching the port, liners pass close to the low, rolling terrain, sprinkled with white, low-rise buildings, clumps of trees poking above. It's a surprisingly soft welcome to the coast of Africa, the wide quaysides punctuated by palms and green shrubs. The terminal is about 40 minutes from Tunis itself and a 20-minute drive from the ancient site of Carthage. To go ashore, non-Europeans will need to retrieve their passports, retained by the ship, to have them stamped by the port authorities.

The heart of Tunis is still the **medina**, the old walled city built by the early Arabic traders. At all the main gates you'll find a large map with all the streets clearly named, and there are small orange signposts pointing the way to the principal sights. The souks have their share of the usual hustlers, so be

---

Tunisia

Climate Summer is long, very hot and dry. Winter is short and mild.
Time Zone GMT+1.
Opening Times These vary according to the time of year and during Ramadan. Shops: 8am–noon, 3–6/7pm; some close on Friday.
Money Matters Dinar, divided into 1,000 millimes.
Festivals and Public Holidays Religious holidays are determined by the lunar calendar and so vary each year. State holidays are fixed: 1 January, 20, 21 March, 9 April, 1 May, 25 July, 13 August.
Etiquette Women should dress with consideration for Muslim sensibilities. Remove shoes before entering mosques. Don't enter at prayers.
Crime and Safety Although crime is not a huge problem, taking valuables into the crowded souk could be risky.
Tipping 10–15 percent for waiters and taxi drivers if on meter (nothing if price agreed beforehand).
Emergency Telephone Numbers Police 197; ambulance 190; fire 198.

wary of anyone offering to show you a view, a museum or a special exhibition; these invariably lead to carpet shops.

The free-standing archway of the **Bab el Bahr** – also called the **Porte de France** (built 1848) – marks the entrance. Walk through it, then take the left-hand of the two narrow alleys facing you. This is the **rue Jemaa ez Zitouna**, the *medina*'s main street, lined with tiny craft shops and souvenir stalls. Here, fragrant incense and exotic perfumes compete with the mouth-watering smell of roasting mutton and the aroma of freshly ground coffee; noises, from the tap-tap-tap of silversmiths' hammers and the scuff of sandalled feet on smooth paving stones, clash with the muezzin's call to prayer from a minaret.

At this point the street disappears into a dark tunnel to emerge at the steps below the door to the **Zitouna Mosque** (literally 'Mosque of the Olive Tree', open daily 8am–noon, closed Fri), the focus of daily life in the *medina* for over one

Stalls line the narrow alleys of the *medina*

thousand years. Visitors are allowed to climb the stairs to an arcade facing the central courtyard, where you can appreciate the tranquillity of the mosque.

The Zitouna Mosque

The most interesting sections of the *medina* are clustered around the walls of the mosque. Centuries ago, these narrow streets were roofed over to provide quarters for the city's craftsmen. Members of high-class guilds such as the booksellers, jewellers and perfumers had the best locations near the mosque, whereas the noisier tradesmen, such as metalworkers and saddlers, were housed some distance away so as not to disturb the scholars studying within. The tanners, with their noxious smells, were banished even further afield to the far side of the city walls. Modern times, and the proliferation of souvenir shops catering to the tourist trade, have brought a breakdown of this strict segregation.

Another of Tunis' highlights is the **Bardo National Museum** (open May–Oct daily 9am–5pm, Nov–Apr 9.30am–4.30pm; admission fee), located in the 19th-century Beyical Palace in western Tunis. It is home to many of Tunisia's greatest archaeological treasures and includes relics from every period of the country's rich history. Among the exhibits are artefacts that may have been related to Punic rituals of child sacrifice rumoured to have been carried out at Carthage, Roman statuary, and a fine baptismal font from the early days of Christianity. The museum's main attraction is its superb collection of Roman mosaics on the first and second floors.

Carthage

Carthage, 18km (11 miles) northeast of Tunis city centre, means 'New Town' in the Phoenician language, and, when the city was founded in 814BC, that's just what it was – a new trading post in the newly emerging maritime empire. Now, it is the oldest city in Tunisia – at least, what little remains. Sacked by the Romans in 146BC, but later rebuilt, this once-great city fell into ruin following the founding of Tunis by the Arabs during the 8th century.

The ancient city was centred on the Hill of Byrsa, on a site now occupied by the **National Museum of Carthage** (open daily Apr–Oct 8am–7pm, Nov–Mar 8.30am–5.30pm; admission fee), which contains an unparalleled collection of Carthaginian artefacts, from all periods. There are also pieces in the adjacent gardens. Beside the museum is an excavation that reveals the walls and foundations of Punic houses five or six storeys high, with water cisterns and drainage channels.

Phoenician ruins, Carthage

Next door, the **Cathedral of St Louis** was built in 1890 on the spot where the King of France, St-Louis, died in 1270 during the 13th crusade. It now houses the **Acropolium** (open daily 9am–6pm), a cultural centre which stages an international festival of classical music every October.

Other ruins include the **Baths of Antoninus Pius**. Dating from the 2nd century AD, these were among the largest in the Roman Empire, covering 3½ hectares (9 acres). A short walk uphill from the baths leads to the **Roman Villas**, a group of ruins including the **odeon**.

Downhill from the odeon, the **Roman Theatre** is almost entirely a 20th-century restoration. Music and drama are staged here during the Carthage International Festival. To the southwest are the **Baths of Gargilius**; further west are the **Cisterns of Malga**, formerly fed by aqueduct from the Zaghouan spring.

> The *tophet* is where for centuries the Carthaginians are rumoured to have sacrificed thousands of their first-born sons to the gods Tanit and Baal Hammon. One school of thought holds that after the victims were strangled, their bones were burned on an altar and the remains buried in urns marked by engraved stone slabs (*stelae*), many of which are shown in the Bardo Museum (*see page 217*).

Sidi-Bou-Saïd

The picture-postcard village of **Sidi-Bou-Saïd** tumbles down a steep slope between its hilltop lighthouse and the sea in a cascade of sugar-cube houses with blue-painted doors and shutters. The village is famous for its unspoilt beauty, the panoramic view from the top of the hill (go all the way up to the lighthouse) and the ornate bird cages made by the locals.

The village is named after a 13th-century holy man who built his mosque and tomb here on the site of an earlier Arab *ribat* (fortified monastery) and lighthouse. Legend has it that St-Louis took refuge here after the sack of Carthage.

The village has two famous cafés – the **Café des Nattes** and the **Café Sidi Chaabane**, both of which offer marvellous views of the village and the sea.

Bizerte

The huge kasbah dominates the Vieux Port at Bizerte

Bizerte has a fine outer harbour linked by canal to two inner harbours. From the entrance to the canal, it's a pleasant walk to the atmospheric old fishing harbour, the **Vieux Port** (Old Port). This is the city's most alluring quarter, its tranquil waters filled with brightly painted fishing boats and lined by white-washed old houses. The harbour entrance is guarded by the massive **kasbah** on one side, and the smaller **Fort el Hani** on the other. The latter houses a small **Oceanographic Museum** and has a pleasant café on the roof.

The hilltop **Fort d'Espagne** (Spanish Fort) above the town is a legacy of Bizerte's pirate past, when the Turkish corsairs would frustrate their pursuers by taking cover within its impregnable walls. At the head of the port, the octagonal minaret of the 17th-century **Great Mosque** is another echo of the Turkish past.

Stretching north from the entrance to the Old Port is the **corniche**, a long, narrow ribbon of golden sand lined with reliable hotels and a number of worthwhile seafood restaurants.

At the tip of the long, sandy peninsula to the east of Bizerte, **Ghar el Melh** is another 17th-century pirate port, complete with a number of Turkish fortresses and mosques. The journey to the nearby *koubba* (dome) of **Sidi Aalu el Mekki** passes alongside a fine beach, and there's yet another beautiful strip of sand at **Raf-Raf**.

LIBYA

Since the lifting of the ban on Americans visiting Libya, cruise lines are rushing to get back into historic Tripoli and the country's second city Benghazi, both essential visits for anyone interested in Roman and Greek history and archaeology.

The Libyans tend to be very friendly and helpful to visitors. The shopping and markets are authentic rather than trashy, and tourists are rarely hassled. Unlike other African and Middle Eastern countries, Libya is one place you don't haggle, making shopping and browsing the souks enjoyable and relaxing.

Tripoli

Tripoli, on the western end of the country's Mediterranean coastline, is a walkable city, heat permitting. Street signs are all in Arabic, but locals are obliging when it comes to giving

Libya

Climate Summer is long, hot and dry. Winter is short and mild.

Time Zone GMT+2 year round.

Opening Times Only approximate opening times can be given since they vary according to the time of year and during Ramadan. Some shops close on Friday (Muslim holy day); 8am–2pm for banks; 9am–2pm and 4.30–8.30pm for shops excluding Friday.

Money Matters Libyan dinar (no credit cards accepted).

Festivals and Public Holidays Religious holidays are determined by the lunar calendar and therefore vary each year. State holidays are fixed: 2 March, 11 July, 1 September.

Etiquette Women should dress with consideration for Muslim sensibilities. Remove shoes before entering mosques; don't enter at prayers.

Tipping Not expected, although hotels may add 10 percent service .

Emergency Telephone Numbers 119 for all services.

directions. The skyline is dominated by the Red Castle, **Al-Saraya al-Hamra**, which sits on the northern promontory overlooking a stretch of reclaimed land leading to the sea. All those who have ruled Tripoli – Turks, Karamanlis, Spaniards, Knights of Malta, Italians and more – have contributed to the castle's structure and contents, which include an impressive library and museum.

The **Jamahiriya Museum** on Green Square, next to the castle, contains one of the most impressive archaeological collections in the Mediterranean region. From here, you can also walk to the *medina* (the Arab old town) and the souk and look for bargains – silver jewellery and leatherware are good buys. Inside the walled city, you'll also find mosques, ancient inns, *hammams* (baths) and traditional houses. Tripoli also has clean, sandy beaches right in front of the city.

Leptis Magna

The main reason for calling at Tripoli, however, is its proximity to **Leptis Magna**, 122km (76 miles) along the coast. Leptis Magna was founded in the first millennium BC and once had a population of 70,000, when it was a successful port exporting grain and olives. The city was eventually engulfed by sand dunes but was initially excavated a century ago to give a fascinating and accurate picture of the Roman Empire in North Africa, with structures as impressive as those in Rome itself.

The theatre is a highlight, with sweeping views over the old city, and you can also visit the market and the double-apsed **Severan Basilica**. The baths complex is the largest built outside Rome, with a sports ground, underfloor heating, hot and cold baths and plunge pools. Most of these buildings were created in the days of the Emperor Septimus Severus, born here in AD146.

Benghazi

Benghazi is Libya's second-largest city, situated on the eastern edge of the Gulf of Sirt. The city is clean and modern, with a lively souk. It is also the gateway city to the beautiful **Green Mountains** (Jebel Akhdar), covered with citrus and olive groves and dotted with small farming towns, not dissimilar to Crete in appearance.

The nearby city of **Cyrene**, another stunning excavation, is one of the best preserved of the Greek cities of Cyrenaica. The city was founded in the 7th century BC, thrived under Roman rule after 96BC, and was abandoned after the Arab conquest in AD642. A visit includes temples, tombs, the *agora*, gymnasium and theatre, rich with mosaics and statues, and the site has a beautiful location on a bluff overlooking the sea. The archaeological dig is still ongoing, and there are not many facilities, so take lots of bottled water.

Leptis Magna

The pyramids at Giza

EGYPT

Egypt's long, illustrious history seems to captivate the modern world. The ancient empire that flourished here from 2500BC until just before the dawn of Christianity was one of the greatest civilisations the world has ever seen. At the beginning of the 19th century, after Napoleon sent his army officers to explore the land and bring back the first hand-drawn impressions of half-buried statues and columns, the world couldn't get enough. When Howard Carter peered through the dusty air of Tutankhamun's tomb in 1922 and, in his own words, 'wonderful things' met his eyes, he confirmed the immeasurable wealth of the pharaohs, and when the backer of the dig, Lord Carnarvon, died suddenly only a few months later, *vox populi* blamed it on the curse of the pharaoh's mummy – and Hollywood was quick to feed our fantasies. Today, pseudo-scientific theories about the origin and purpose of the pyramids abound. Our interest and curiosity about Egypt is, it seems, insatiable.

Port Said

By Egyptian standards, **Port Said** is in its infancy, not founded until 1859 when work began on the Suez Canal. Many parts of the city are even younger, having been rebuilt following bombing raids during the Suez Crisis in 1956 and Egypt's wars with Israel in the 1960s and 1970s. While not a major tourist destination in its own right, Port Said is a free port and offers some of the best shopping in Egypt. It also has uncrowded beaches, some decent restaurants, museums (notably its National Museum, which has exhibits from every period of Egyptian history, and a Military Museum) and pretty public gardens.

Port Said, together with Alexandria *(see page 229)*, is the main gateway for ocean-cruise passengers wishing to visit Cairo, the pyramids at Giza and the Sphinx. Full-day trips take in all three.

Egypt

Climate Long, hot, dry summers and short, mild winters.

Time Zone GMT+2.

Opening Times Times vary according to the time of year, particularly during Ramadan. Some shops close on Friday (Muslim holy day). Banks open 8.30am–1.30pm.

Money Matters Pounds.

Festivals and Public Holidays Religious holidays are determined by the lunar calendar and therefore vary each year. State holidays are fixed: 1 January, 25 April, 1 May, 23 July, 6 October.

Etiquette Women should dress with consideration for Muslim sensibilities. Remove shoes before entering mosques. Don't enter during prayers.

Tipping 10 percent for restaurant waiters if service is not included; 1–5 pounds for a taxi driver.

Emergency Telephone Numbers Police 122; ambulance 123; fire 125.

Cairo

Founded in 641 and expanded by the Fatimids in the 9th century, **Cairo** (Al-Qahira or 'the Victorious') became the most powerful Islamic city of the medieval era. Located where the Nile valley widens into its delta, it is now the largest city in Africa, with a population of over 16 million. The heat, dust and noise are constant, but it's a fascinating place to visit.

A day tour usually includes a trip to the **Egyptian Museum of Antiquities** (open daily 9am–4.45pm; admission fee), home to some of ancient Egypt's finest treasures. Many of the most admired items are on the second floor, where over 1,700 objects found at Tutankhamun's tomb by Howard Carter in 1922 are on display. Three coffins surrounding the king's mummy are housed here; the inner one, made of pure gold, weighs 170kg (374lb).

In the Mummy Room, also upstairs, you can admire the preserved remains of some of Egypt's most illustrious rulers.

Shimmering interior of the 'Alabaster Mosque', Cairo

Dating mainly from the 18th to the 20th dynasties, they include Ramesses IV, Seti I and Tuthmosis III. Tutankhamun is not among them: the Egyptian authorities decided he should be returned to his tomb in Valley of the Kings.

Other highlights include its **Citadel**, built in the early 13th century to protect the city from Crusaders. Its centrepiece is the fabulous

Typical decorative motif, Citadel

19th-century **Muhammad Ali Mosque**. The largest mosque in the city, it has earned the name 'Alabaster Mosque' for its grand interior faced with the smooth pale stone.

Giza and the Pyramids

Archaeologists agree that the **pyramids at Giza** were built within a few hundred years of each other c.2600BC by generations of the same royal family, with the aim of foiling tomb robbers. The largest of the three, the **Great Pyramid of Khufu**, is the only survivor of the Seven Wonders of the World described by Greek and Roman scholars. It stands 137m (450ft) high and was the tallest structure in the world until 1898 when the Eiffel Tower was built in Paris. Inside, steep, narrow tunnels lead to a tiny funerary chamber containing a simple granite sarcophagus. Even more remarkable is the ventilation system: astronomers have proved that the air shafts are aligned with major constellations in the skies of ancient Egypt.

The **Pyramid of Khafre** is smaller than the Great Pyramid, though its location on slightly higher ground makes it appear taller. A red granite sarcophagus was found in the interior chamber. The smallest pyramid, **Menkaure**, adds a wonderful perspective to the alignment of the three pyramids. To the south of this are three smaller, unfinished pyramids thought to be for the family of Menkaure.

The three pharaohs were not the only ones laid to rest at Giza, the site of a royal burial ground from the days of the Old Kingdom. The desert landscape is dotted with mud-brick tombs and *mastabas* (stone tombs with flat roofs), although they are not as impressive as the pyramids themselves.

Seated at the base of the sacred causeway that once linked the pyramids to the Nile is the **Sphinx**, the enigmatic depiction of Khafre with his head attached to a lion's body. In Egyptian mythology, sphinxes were guardian deities, and this was monumental protection, at an impressive 73m (240ft) long and 20m (66ft) high. Following Khafre's death, the body of the Sphinx was progressively buried by desert sand. Tuthmosis IV believed that the statue spoke to him, telling him he would become pharaoh if he cleared the sand away – which he hastened to do. From then on, ancient Egyptians believed the monument had prophetic powers.

The Sphinx and Great Pyramid

You can tour the pyramids on foot, camel or horseback. The pyramids are open daily 8am–4pm, 5pm in summer. Access to the interior of Khufu is limited to 150 people only in the morning and 150 in the afternoon.

Alexandria

Alexandria, built in 331BC on the orders of Alexander the
Great, had been a port (known as Rhatokis) used by the
pharaohs as far back as the 9th century BC. But it was as
Alexandria that it made its name as one of the most important
cities of the ancient world, home to one of its Seven Wonders
– the Lighthouse – and one of the world's greatest libraries,
containing more than half a million books and manuscripts.

The city is a popular base for eastern Mediterranean cruise
itineraries, offering access to Cairo and the pyramids at Giza
(see page 227) but also worth exploring in its own right.

The broad boulevard bordering Alexandria's waterfront is
the corniche. Close by is Alexandria's main souk, an atmospheric one-stop-shop for everything from spices to patterned
rugs. A stroll along the corniche is the medieval **Qaytbay Fort**
(open daily May–Oct 9am–4pm and 5–11pm, winter 9am–
5.30pm; admission fee), built on the site of the ancient **Pharos**
(lighthouse) and housing some relics from the original.

The **Graeco-Roman Museum** (open daily 9am–5pm; admission fee) has exhibits dating from the 3rd century BC, while
Pompey's Pillar, more than 27m (80ft) high and made of rose-
pink granite, was erected in AD297 and is perhaps Alexandria's
best-known Roman monument. Alexandria also has Egypt's
only Roman amphitheatre, which was excavated in the 1960s
and has glittering white marble terraces. Now there are hopes
of excavating something even more remarkable – Cleopatra's
palace – from the seabed off Alexandria's coast; vast columns
and statues have already been recovered. The excavations at
Kom al-Dikkah (open daily 9am–5pm; admission fee) and the
Graeco-Roman Museum are on most visitors' sightseeing list.

Many of the city's best beaches are accessible from the
corniche, the broad boulevard bordering Alexandria's waterfront, which is lined with imposing, grand 19th-century hotels – a good choice for lunch with a view of the bay.

HANDY TRAVEL TIPS

A Summary of Practical Information

CHOOSING A CRUISE

Picking the right ship and itinerary is critical to the success of a cruise holiday. Don't assume that all ships are the same, or that all itineraries are identical. A cruise might, for example, include several days at sea, or a port a day, with sailing only at night. Some ships overnight in certain ports for the nightlife, or for extended shore excursions. Others cram two ports into one day.

For a full list, descriptions and contact details of cruise lines operating in the Mediterranean, *see pages 250–3*.

For a detailed description of every aspect of the cruising experience, plus money-saving tips and exhaustive reviews of more than 250 cruise ships, we recommend the *Berlitz Guide to Ocean Cruising & Cruise Ships* by Douglas Ward, published annually.

The range of cruises on offer has greatly increased in recent years, and it is now possible to take just about any type of cruise in the Mediterranean. The mega-ships of Princess Cruises and Royal Caribbean offer the whole big-ship experience, from Broadway shows and a host of dining options to numerous deck sports and a high proportion of balcony cabins. SeaDream Yacht Club and Seabourn are at the other end of the scale, providing a setting similar to a large, very luxurious, private yacht. Star Clippers, Sea Cloud, Peter Deilmann's *Lili Marleen* and Windstar Cruises are the ships to choose for the romance of a sailing ship, whether it's a square rigger or a fully automated gin palace. And for the cost-conscious, Thomson, Island Cruises and Ocean Village provide great cruise-and-stay offers and seven-night itineraries out of Palma, Mallorca and other popular ports. Meanwhile, Costa Cruises and Italian-owned MSC have big, modern ships and a more international flavour than the British or US-run vessels. Ships belonging to P&O and Fred Olsen, on the other hand, will carry mainly Brits. And, for the more independently-minded, cost-conscious traveller, there's the recently launched easyCruise.com.

CABINS

Once you've decided on your ship, there's then the choice of what type of cabin to opt for. The choice is between an inside cabin, outside cabin, balcony cabin or suite. Specific cabins can be prebooked on all ships, although some cruise lines charge for this.

Choosing an inside cabin, particularly on a lower deck, is the cheapest way to cruise. Balcony cabins are more and more commonplace and offer the luxury of private sunbathing. Some ships (such as Royal Caribbean's Radiance Class vessels) have extra-deep balconies at the aft end, which are better still.

When booking, bear in mind the direction in which the ship is travelling; from Genoa to Barcelona, for example, the views will all be on the starboard side. Anyone worried about seasickness should opt for a cabin on a lower deck, near the more stable centre of the ship. Ironically, the suites are always at the top and will get the roughest ride in choppy seas. They do, however, often come with butler service, dining privileges and red-carpet treatment.

CRUISING WITH CHILDREN

Some ships are more suitable than others for families. Generally speaking, the larger and newer the ship, the better the facilities. P&O, Princess, Carnival, NCL and Royal Caribbean are all excellent, with superb playrooms for all ages from tots to teenagers, and creative activity programmes. Cunard's QM2 and QE2 have nurseries staffed by Norland nannies. Celebrity and Holland America Line offer good childcare in peak season, while Ocean Village has the best facilities of the budget cruise lines. Costa and MSC's big new ships are also family-orientated, although the child carers may be Italian and the other children of varying nationalities.

It used to be the case that parents could not go ashore and leave their offspring in the children's club, but this has changed, with some ships providing day-long care. Exhausted parents of babies and toddlers should consider a ship with a night nursery, so that they can dine alone while their children are cared for. But don't just plan to dump children in a playroom – one of the joys of cruising is that you can make short forays into interesting ports as a family and retire to the ship when it gets too hot.

HOME PORTS

Some ships (generally the more upmarket ones) roam continually, so you'll board in, say, Athens and disembark in Istanbul, where the next passengers will board, disembarking in Venice, and so on. Other ships operate out of one home port for the entire season, sailing seven night loops, usually with a couple of variations for those who want to book holidays lasting two weeks. So you might sail out of Palma, Mallorca, around the French and Spanish coasts in week one and back to Palma, departing for Tunisia in week two.

There are several home ports in the Mediterranean. They are big enough for the ships to dock, rather than tender, and are always in cities with international airports. Many of these airports are served nowadays by low-cost airlines, so you could book your own flights to save money.

Palma is one of the most popular home ports, used by British cruise lines Thomson, Island and Ocean Village, who bring passengers in by charter flight and sell hotel add-ons after their cruises. Venice is another major home port, and many cruise lines will give you an overnight in port there before sailing the next day.

Athens is the base for ships cruising the Aegean and Turkish coast, with a few cruise lines using Istanbul, which, with its dramatic approach along the Bosphorus, is a very exciting city in which to start and finish a cruise. In the western Mediterranean, Barcelona is hugely popular as a home port; its large port can take several big ships at once and you will often see five or six large ships lined up there. If your cruise turns around in Barcelona and you're not on the cruise line's charter flight, book a late flight out so you get a day in the city at the end of your trip. Naples,

Civitavecchia (the port for Rome) and Cannes (for smaller ships) are also used as turnaround ports.

Southampton and Dover are the start and finish points for many P&O, Cunard and Fred Olsen cruises, with Royal Caribbean and Princess also basing ships in Southampton in the summer now. It's a long haul down to the Mediterranean from these British ports (two or three days to cross the Bay of Biscay and enter the Mediterranean at Gibraltar) but for UK-based cruise passengers who prefer not to fly, these voyages are ideal. Again, if you're travelling from the US, add on an extra day or two either to explore London or the nearby Hampshire or Kent countryside.

TRAVELLERS WITH DISABILITIES

Cruising is an ideal form of travel for travellers with disabilities. All new ships are built with cabins suitable for wheelchair users, as well as lifts able to take wheelchairs and ramps at the doors, both on the ship and leading out to the deck. Lift buttons and signs are usually in Braille, and some theatres are adapted with headphones for the hard of hearing. The key to success is to book early, as the wheelchair-adapted cabins tend to go quickly, and to check over the arrangements for airport transfers and boarding the ship very thoroughly with your travel agent. Note that if the sea is choppy, the crew may not be able to get wheelchair users onto the ship's tenders for safety reasons, so choose a cruise with as few tender ports as possible (these are indicated in the brochure).

WEDDINGS

Because of legal issues, few ships' captains will conduct an actual wedding (although the captains of *Golden*, *Grand* and *Star Princess* are allowed to because of the ships' registration). But anybody bringing along a vicar, priest or rabbi can get married on a ship, either in port or at sea. Many cruise lines, including Holland America Line, Princess and P&O, have wedding packages and wedding co-ordinators; some vessels have wedding chapels, although for some reason, these tend to be rather joyless, often without windows. Ask if you can have the ceremony on the bridge instead. Also, remember to book hair and make-up arrangements for the bride as soon as you board the ship.

An alternative is to marry ashore and honeymoon on a ship; or to marry and have a reception on the ship in port, and then sail off into the sunset on honeymoon. Many cruise lines also offer 'renewal of vows' packages, which are increasingly popular.

PREPARING FOR THE TRIP

From booking agents and money considerations to passport requirements and what to take with you on the cruise, this section includes information to help you prepare for your holiday afloat.

BOOKING

Booking Agents in the UK

There is a vast choice of Mediterranean cruises for people from the UK, some aimed directly at the UK market and packaged as fly-cruises and some operating from UK ports. Look for a travel agent affiliated to PSARA, the Passenger Shipping Association Retail Agent Scheme, <www.psa-psara.org>. The following is just a selection of agents:

• **Cruise Control** Stanton Gate, 49 Mawney Road, Romford, RM7 7HL, tel: 0870 909 7540; <www.cruisecontrol cruises.co.uk>.

• **The Cruise People** 88 York Street, W1H 1QT, tel: 020 7723 2450 or 0800 526 313; <www.cruisepeople.co.uk>.

• **Cumbria Cruise Club** Andrews Court, Andrews Way, Barrow-in-Furness, LA14 2UD, tel: 0800 003 002, <www.cumbriacruise.com>

• **Marion Owen Travel** 23 Portland Street, Hull, HU2 8JX, tel: 01482 212525; <www.marionowentravel.com>.

• **Mundy Cruising** Quadrant House, 80–2 Regent Street, London W1R 6JB, tel: 020 7734 4404; <www.mundycruising.co.uk>.

• **Premier Travel** 10 Rose Crescent, Cambridge, CB2 3LL, tel: 0870 040 8080, <www.premiertravelagency.co.uk>.
• **Voyana** 4 Buckingham Parade, The Broadway, Stanmore, HA7 4EB, tel: 0871 271 5490, <www.worldcruisedirect.com>.

Booking Agents in the US

Some European cruise holidays are sold as fly-cruises but it is possible to buy 'cruise only' trip and make separate flight arrangements. The main European gateways for cruises are Athens, Barcelona, Istanbul, Lisbon, London and Rome. Book a cruise through an agent accredited by the Cruise Line International Association (CLIA), <www.cruising.org>. Here is a selection of agents:
• **Cruise Holidays** has stores all over the US and Canada, tel: 800-866 7245; <www.cruiseholidays.com>.
• **Cruise Planners** has stores in Florida and California, tel: 866-418 5672; <www.cruiseplannersforyou.com>.
• **Liberty Travel** has over 200 stores all over the East Coast, tel: 1-888-271 1584; <www.libertytravel.com>.
• **Cruise.com** claims to be the world's largest seller of cruises on the web, tel: 888-333 3116; <www.cruise.com>.
• **Cruises Inc.** is one of the largest online agents, with a vast pool of specialists nationwide, tel: 866-280 8198. All their agents are listed on <www.cruisesinc.com>.

BUDGETING

Theoretically, you don't have to spend any money once you've boarded your ship, although you probably will unless you stick to the bare essentials. Budget for drinks and personal extras on board, shore excursions and spending money when in port. You can save money by eating a big breakfast, missing lunch ashore and feasting on afternoon tea back on board. You can also save by organising your own shore excursions, with some careful planning. Check with your travel agent which currency is used on board – usually either US dollars or euros.

Hidden Extras Items *included* in the price of your cruise are as follows: all food; all entertainment; use of most gym and sports facilities (but not always all of them); transfers from the port (usually); port taxes; room service (sometimes); shuttle buses into town (sometimes); flights (usually); use of the ship's self-service laundry (usually); use of the ship's library; captain's cocktail party (if there is one).

Items *not included* are: alcoholic drinks (except on Silversea, Seabourn, SeaDream Yacht Club, Seven Seas Cruises and Hebridean Island Cruises); tips (unless stated); travel insurance; spa treatments; shore excursions (except on Hebridean Island Cruises and Swan Hellenic); medical care; internet access and telephone calls from the satellite phone. Some cruise lines also charge extra for: bridge visits; use of some sports equipment on board; 'premium' exercise classes such as yoga; mineral water in cabins; room service; tea and coffee; and shuttle buses. Most charge extra for dining in the 'alternative' restaurants.

Note that no extras are included in the price with easyCruise.com, except for your bed and bathroom – even food has to be paid for on board.

Tax The cost of port taxes will usually be included in the cruise fare, as will airport taxes. Many European countries charge a version of Value Added Tax (VAT). This sales tax is usually included in the price (unlike some US states, where the tax is added as you pay). In some countries, such as Spain, there are different levels of tax. Anyone living outside the EU is entitled to a tax refund on items bought in the EU; claim this at any port or airport where there is a Global Refund office (listed on <www.globalrefund.com>).

Tipping on Board These are not usually included in the fare but do check; on Silversea, Hebridean Island Cruises and SeaDream Yacht Club, they are included. Elsewhere, it is expected that passengers tip their waiter, cabin steward and sundry others (who may not have played a role in serving you). A 15 percent 'gratuity' is often added to all drinks purchases, especially on ships aimed at US passengers.

Tips may be added automatically to your on-board account. Some cruise lines place envelopes in the cabins on the final evening. There is no obligation to pay using either method if you are not happy with the service, although it helps all concerned if you take any complaints up with the hotel manager on board. Some people take a view that the staff are not paid very much and depend on tips; others prefer to reward only those who have helped them personally. Others are of the opinion that they should not be responsible for paying the crew's wages. In addition to a tip, the biggest favour you can do for a ship's employee is to write a grateful letter to their manager.

HEALTH AND MEDICAL MATTERS

Health Insurance EU citizens are entitled to free emergency hospital treatment with a European Health Insurance Card (replacing the old form E111). Private health insurance is strongly advisable – with some cruise lines, it is a prerequisite to booking.

Insects Mosquitoes are generally only a nuisance in port in the evening. To combat them, pack a plentiful supply of insect repellent. Wasps are common in July and August. Small scorpions may be encountered in rural areas, but they are still pretty rare. Wasp and jellyfish stings can be treated with over-the-counter remedies.

Medication and Prescriptions Travellers should bring supplies of any medication they use, as the ship's doctor will not be able to provide it. It is always sensible to bring along copies of any prescriptions – whether for medication or contact lenses and glasses – in case of emergency.

Sun Protection It's all too easy to relax by the pool, lulled into a false sense of security by a cooling sea breeze. But the Mediterranean sun is very strong, and the reflection off the sea can increase its intensity. Bring a high-factor sunscreen and wear it whenever you go out. For starters, expose your skin to the sun for brief periods only, preferably in the morning or late afternoon when the sun's rays are least intense. As your tan builds, you can increase your sunbathing time and decrease your protection factor – though you will still need protection. Bring a brimmed hat, especially if you plan to do any extended hiking, walking, or playing in the midday sun.

Vaccinations There are few health risks in the Mediterranean, although a typhoid vaccination is recommended for some North African countries. Excesses of sun or alcohol, or contaminated water, are the most likely causes of illness.

PASSPORTS AND VISAS

On a cruise, you give up your passport on boarding the ship and only collect it on the last day. Usually, cruise lines will obtain group visas for all passengers where appropriate and permits are handed out if people want to go ashore. Some countries require individuals to apply for visas, in which case the cruise line/travel agent will advise. Sometimes, cruise lines will not be able to obtain group visas for holders of certain passports, in which case it is the responsibility of the passenger to get their own visa before departure.

WHEN TO GO

The Mediterranean/European cruise season starts in April and extends until early November, although some lines are now operating Christmas/New Year cruises. July and August are peak season, and ports can be both hot and crowded at this time. May, June and September are ideal for cooler weather and fewer crowds.

Very few ships operate exclusively in the Mediterranean year-round; Costa, Fred Olsen, MSC, P&O and Thomson have ships in Europe throughout the year, but they tend to spend the winter season in the Canary Islands.

WHAT TO TAKE

Study the itinerary carefully; it will tell you how many 'formal' nights to expect. For these, the dress code is black tie. 'Informal' means cocktail dresses (lounge suits for men), and 'casual' means smart resort clothes. Be aware that cruise lines that may have formal nights in, say, Alaska, may drop this policy in the hot Mediterranean summer.

Bring swimwear, walking shoes (for excursions), deck shoes, a gym kit if you plan to work out, lots of sunblock, a sun hat, spare film/memory flash cards for your camera (expensive on board), binoculars, small umbrella, walking pole/collapsible shooting stick if you're less mobile; a rucksack (day pack); seasickness remedies; and any regular medication you need – the ship's doctor should not be expected to supply this. Remember to bring a driving licence and photo ID if you think you'll want to hire a vehicle for an independent tour.

And what about what *not* to take…Items you don't need to pack include masses of books – get them from the ship's library instead *(see page 241)*; duty-free drink (it will be confiscated and stored for you on some cruises); unnecessary sharp objects or anything that resembles a weapon (they may be confiscated).

LIFE ON BOARD

Ship designers are constantly pushing the limits of entertainment at sea. Modern ships may offer anything from ice skating to mini golf and a climbing wall up the funnel. Also expect basketball courts, nightclubs with rotating dance floors and, most recently, a planetarium (on the QM2, for example). On the other hand, a small ship may simply have one elegant bar and a library.

ACTIVITIES AND ENTERTAINMENT

Art Auctions Don't expect to find Old Masters in the ship's art auction. While the auction itself may be fun, a lot of the art is tacky. Serious buyers should research galleries in the ports of call instead.

Board Games Ships usually carry a range of board games; a tradition is to have a large jigsaw puzzle on display for general amusement. Many vessels have dedicated card rooms offering bridge sessions.

Casinos Most modern cruise ships have a casino. On some, it is the hub of activity, while on others it is tucked away discreetly. Some cruise lines, such as Crystal, ply gamblers with free drinks, and the casinos are lively late into the night.

The daytime gambling lessons offered by cruise lines are fun and informative; usually, ships' casinos are friendly and informal compared to those ashore, although they are governed by the same rules. Just remember to set yourself a budget and to know when to stop.

Ships' casinos are closed when the ship is in port, but there are some fine casinos ashore around the Mediterranean for serious players, in places such as Cannes, Marbella, Monaco and Palma. Take a passport to get in and dress appropriately.

Film and Television All ships offer in-cabin TV, usually showing satellite channels, films and the ship's own channels, be it shopping talks or televised lectures. Many ships have a cinema, too, showing first-run movies. Some have free video and DVD libraries.

Lectures Many ships carry guest lecturers who will speak on topics related to the cruising area, from marine biology to Moorish architecture. The lectures are free and are often broadcast on the ship's TV channel.

Library Facilities The ship's library provides a quiet on-board retreat and an endless source of free reading material, from novels to atlases and guidebooks. Ships attracting an international audience have books in German, French, Spanish and Italian as well as English.

Most ships carry a selection of magazines in the library. 'Newspapers' are provided by satellite link, condensed, printed out and delivered directly to cabins. This tradition continues, despite the fact that the internet and satellite TV make it much easier for passengers to keep up to date with world events.

Live Music Ships nowadays offer everything from concert pianists to scantily clad, all-female string quartets. Some have great tribute bands (to Madonna, or The Beatles, for example), talented jazz musicians and excellent orchestras.

Shows Big 'production' shows can be spellbinding at sea, with new ships having technical facilities on a par with those of a London or Broadway theatre. Big-name musicals, futuristic circus shows (including trapeze acts) and opera have all been staged on ships.

COMMUNICATIONS

Internet Cruise passengers are advised to set up a webmail account before leaving home. It is cheaper and more reliable than sending and receiving emails via the ship's system.

Telephones Telephoning from a ship's satellite system is expensive. It is much cheaper to make calls from a land line in port, or even from a mobile phone with a roaming agreement – when the ship is at sea you are usually out of range of mobile/cellphone transmitters. Internet access is offered on practically all ships, at varying prices, either per minute or per kilobyte (kb).

ETIQUETTE

Bridge Visits These are rarely possible because of security reasons, although a very small cruise ship such as those operated by Star Clippers, SeaDream Yacht Club and Hebridean Island Cruises may have an 'open bridge' policy, when you can visit at most times of day. This usually excludes arriving in and departing from ports, when a pilot is on board.

Captain and Crew If you are invited to dine with the captain, consider it an honour and reply immediately. Observe the dress code for the evening and don't be late.

Do not expect to befriend the crew in order to be invited to the crew bar. This is their private space – and they don't get much of it. The ship will also not be insured for passengers straying out of the passenger areas and whoever takes you there could get into serious trouble.

Fellow Passengers If you are unhappy with your dining companions on board, ask the maître d' discreetly if you can be moved – many people do. And the earlier you ask, the better.

If someone is hogging a sunlounger with unclaimed belongings, move them and claim the lounger for yourself, provided you are prepared to accept the same treatment.

Don't be shocked if fellow passengers ask how much you paid for your cruise. In today's competitive market, many people consider it a sport to shop around. You don't have to tell them, of course.

Smoking On most ships nowadays, public areas (except cigar bars) are non-smoking – a rule that must be observed. If you hate smoking, and the person in the next-door cabin puffs smoke over your balcony, there is little you can do other than ask to be moved.

FOOD AND DRINK

To say that you can eat round the clock on a cruise is no exaggeration, so dine in moderation to avoid being winched off as freight. Unless there is a 'speciality' restaurant on board, all the food on a cruise is included in the price. Silversea, Seabourn, Hebridean Island, Radisson and SeaDream Yacht Club all include drinks as well (wine only on Radisson).

Bars Ships' bars can be fun, elegant and atmospheric, ranging from sophisticated martini bars and club-like cigar rooms to Irish theme pubs. Champagne bars are currently in vogue; the QM2 has one, as do some of the Royal Caribbean ships. All drinks bought in the bar can be signed for. Be aware that many ships will add an automatic 'gratuity' of 15 percent.

Cafés The queues at speciality coffee shops are testament to the fact that cruise-ship tea and coffee are generally awful, although most modern ships have cappuccino/espresso machines. Many ships combine coffee shops with internet terminals. More traditional passengers may prefer afternoon tea, which is often offered with white-glove service, dainty cakes and sandwiches with the crusts cut off.

Restaurants All ships have a main dining room; many have speciality restaurants (Italian, Japanese, Mexican and Mediterranean being just some examples), where a small premium is usually charged for a different menu and more exclusive surroundings. Book these early, as reservations go quickly. Some of these restaurants are outstanding.

Some ships offer from two to four different dinner sittings in the dining room, while others have 'open seating', meaning that you eat when you like and sit wherever you want. All ships also offer a casual dining option, which is popular in the Mediterranean in summer if it permits dining alfresco on deck. Don't miss the themed buffets, which are often spectacular.

Vegetarians, vegans and any other dietary requirements are usually well catered for. If in doubt, check with the cruise line.

Room Service This is usually included in the cost of the cruise, although some lower-budget cruise lines either charge for it or do not offer it. Service will range from the decadence of a five-star ship, on which passengers can order *filet migon* and caviar in the middle of the night if they wish, to a more basic menu. Many ships, particularly those catering to British people, now have tea- and coffee-making facilities in the cabins.

HEALTH AND HYGIENE

All cruise ships have a doctor and nurse on board (the exception being cargo ships or private yachts carrying fewer than 12 people, as these are not required to have a doctor). Facilities vary from ship to ship, but a doctor should be able to treat most ailments, including heart attacks and appendicitis. Seriously ill passengers may be stabilised until the ship arrives in port, or airlifted off. There will always be a fee for consulting the ship's doctor, although many ships hand out sea-sickness tablets free of charge. Passengers should, however, bring their own supplies of any medication they use, as the ship's doctor will not be able to provide it.

Norovirus (a common gastro-intestinal virus) occurs on cruise ships, as it does in hospitals and hotels, and it can spread quickly. If you have diarrhoea, vomiting and fever, report to the ship's doctor immediately. Avoid the virus by using the antiseptic hand wipes that are handed out on board and by washing hands scrupulously.

Drinking Water If you are prone to stomach upsets, it is best to avoid drinking tap water, although it is generally clean and perfectly safe in Mediterranean countries. Bottled water should be readily available everywhere. Drinking water on cruise ships is heavily chlorinated and while safe, does not taste particularly nice – this perhaps explains why cruise-ship tea and coffee often tastes so peculiar. All ships provide bottled water, although many charge for it.

MONEY MATTERS

Cruise operators encourage guests to register a credit card at the beginning of a voyage for on-board expenses. Otherwise, a bill will be compiled to be settled on the day of departure. While on board, whether a credit card is registered or not, everything is paid for using a special card issued by the ship.

There is usually a cash machine on board near the shops or casino, and exchange facilities at the customer-relations desk, but rates are not competitive, so it's recommended that you use a local bank in port instead. For shore visits, bring credit or charge cards for large purchases and a supply of euros for France, Greece, Italy, Portugal and Spain; euros are also accepted in Croatia, Malta and Tunisia.

For countries outside the eurozone, you can change money on the ship (at a hefty premium) or look for an ATM ashore. Most modern cruise terminals have at least one ATM.

Cashing travellers cheques can be inconvenient when you are on a shore excursion or have limited time in port, although they are a secure way to keep your money.

RELIGIOUS SERVICES

Interdenominational services are held on most ships, conducted either by the captain, staff captain, or an on-board chaplain. Special Jewish charters will usually have a rabbi on board; some offer kosher food.

You can attend services in churches or mosques in port if you are dressed appropriately. Women and non-Muslim men should not expect to attend a service in a mosque. The local tourist board will have details of services in the area.

SPORTS FACILITIES AND SPAS

Deck Games Paddle tennis (using a slightly smaller tennis court than is usual) is hugely popular at sea. A paddle tennis court will usually double up as a volleyball/basketball court. Most ships offer deck quoits and shuffleboard, the traditional cruising games. Also look out for golf-driving nets and putting greens, jogging tracks, climbing walls and table tennis.

Gyms Most ships have gyms with modern equipment – sometimes more impressive than you'll find on shore. Most also run exercise classes, although a premium is usually charged for fashionable classes such as yoga and pilates.

Spas Spas at sea are now winning awards over land-based retreats. Many ships' spas are run by Steiner (includes the Mandara brand), with a couple of exceptions, among them the Parisian Carita concessions on Radisson Seven Seas' ships. Anything from hot-rock massage to massage for couples and 'chakra balancing' is offered – at a price. Rates are adjusted to match the demographics of the passengers, so expect to pay a premium on an upmarket ship.

Swimming Pools and Hot Tubs All ships offer at least one salt-water pool and a hot tub on deck; some have three or four pools, multiple hot tubs and water slides. Several vessels have a retractable roof over a second pool for cooler weather. The pool will be emptied when seas are rough.

Watersports Smaller ships may have a retractable watersports platform, which is lowered for swimming, windsurfing, banana boat rides, waterskiing and dinghy sailing. All the equipment is carried on board and is usually free of charge. Large ships may have arrangements with local hotels in the Mediterranean for the use of watersports equipment. Several vessels also carry a dive boat and their own scuba equipment.

LIFE ASHORE

After perhaps days at sea, time ashore at a Mediterranean port is to be savoured. Ancient ruins, museums, shops and markets are all on offer, as are new smells, sounds and tastes. Exploring independently can be an adventure, and not too much of a challenge for experienced travellers. Organised excursions are normally a more expensive option, but most cruise lines strive to provide a high standard of tour.

INDEPENDENT TOURS

There are numerous ways to get around in the Mediterranean, from walking to cycling, hiring a powerboat, car, taxi or moped for the day, or taking ferry, local bus or train. Remember to bring a driving licence and photo ID for hiring any vehicle; note also that driving is on the right across Continental Europe, and drivers are often fairly aggressive. If you are walking, remember that drivers do not automatically stop at pedestrian crossings.

Research the destination thoroughly before you arrive and take a good map. Always check that train, bus and ferry times coincide with the ship's arrival and departure (for example, the hydrofoil from Sorrento to Capri). Make reservations for particularly special lunch venues and check that important museums and galleries are open; many close for one day a week, and perhaps for a couple of hours at lunchtime. Plan shopping trips to avoid the heat of the day and early-afternoon shop closures.

Joining forces with other passengers and hiring a minibus or a large taxi is often cost-effective, but do establish the fare first.

Remember that it is your responsibility to get back to the ship on time and if you miss it, to catch up with it at the next port.

ORGANISED EXCURSIONS

Shore excursions represent a major cost on any cruise, and are an important source of income for the cruise line (apart from Swan Hellenic and Hebridean Island Cruises, which include shore excursions in their fares). Passengers are encouraged to book in advance, which can be done online with some cruise lines. Popular excursions do sell out, but don't feel pressurised to book everything before boarding the ship; a couple of days off may be welcome on an intensive Mediterranean itinerary. Try to find a good balance – for example, book ahead for the things you know you'll definitely want to do, and take pot luck on board for the rest; your decision once on board may be influenced by weather, how active or lazy you're feeling and recommendations from other passengers.

A shore excursion will provide an overview of a new place, or greater detail on a specific site, such as Pompeii, in Italy, or Ephesus, in Turkey. It may be an opportunity to try a new sport, for example kayaking or mountain biking, in a group. If you want to linger in a gallery, or dedicate the day to shopping or a long lunch, go it alone. Shore tours do have free time built in, but it will be limited, and you will sometimes be taken to shopping places you wouldn't otherwise have chosen, such as out-of-the-way pottery or carpet showrooms.

Shore excursions vary greatly in price, from around $20 to $45 for a city sightseeing orientation to over $300 for a full day, including entrance to various sites and, for that price, a decent lunch. They are usually priced in US dollars, or on P&O, Fred Olsen and Ocean Village and other British lines, in sterling. Very occasionally, excursions will be priced in euros.

Many cruise lines, particularly at the top end, now organise special 'experiences', for example, a private motor launch to tour the canals of Venice ($150) or Crystal Cruises' rather spectacular helicopter sightseeing from Naples, flying low over Vesuvius, Pompeii, Herculaneum and landing on the jetset island of Capri for lunch; roughly around $2,000 for the day.

Booking Shore Excursions There are various ways to book these excursions. As already mentioned, many cruise lines (Crystal, NCL and Royal Caribbean/Celebrity, for example) allow – and even prefer – you to book online before you leave; some cruise lines send out pamphlets for pre-booking. You can also book onboard at the excursion desk, although there is often a long queue for this on embarkation day. Consult the ship's daily programme to see when bookings close for various tours; this is usually a couple of days before the event, as the cruise line has to give numbers to its ground agent.

Booking ahead has its advantages, saving hassle when you arrive, but do be warned that if, for example, a port of call is dropped, or if you're ill and don't go, it may be a struggle to get your money back. Pay by credit card so that you can reclaim if necessary from your card issuer.

CRUISE LINES

• **Costa Cruises** UK: 5 Gainsford Street, London SE1 2NE, tel: 020 7940 4499; <www.costacruises.co.uk>; US: World Trade Center, 80 SW 8th Street, 27th Floor, Miami, FL 33130-3097, tel: 800-447 6877/305-358 7325; <www.costacruises.com>. Italian-run subsidiary of Carnival Corporation. Fleet of mixed age including some large modern ships ideally suited to Mediterranean cruising. Passengers are of mixed nationalities (including many Italians) and are of all ages.

• **Crystal Cruises** UK: Quadrant House, 80–2 Regent Street, London W1B 5JB, tel: 020 7287 9040; US: 2049 Century Park East, Suite 1400, Los Angeles, CA 90067, tel: 800-804 1500; <www.crystalcruises.com>. Large, elegant ships sailing the world (Europe in summer) and offering a luxurious experience in a big-ship setting.

• **Cunard Line** UK: Richmond House, Terminus Terrace, Southampton SO14 3PN, tel: 0845 071 0300; <www.cunard.co.uk>; US: 24305 Town Center Drive, Santa Clarita, CA 91355, tel: 800-728 6273. Cunard operates cruises from the UK and fly-cruises in the Mediterranean.

• **easyCruise.com** The most recent addition to the easyeverything empire. Offers flexible week-long cruises along the French and Italian Rivieras, the only stipulation being that a minimum of two nights only must be spent on the ship. Aimed at independently minded travellers on a budget. Stops at St-Tropez, Cannes, Nice, Monaco, Imperia (for San Remo), Genoa and Portofino, with connecting easyJet flights available Nice and Genoa. Cabins are minimalist, ie basic, but extremely well priced to match.

• **Fred Olsen Cruise Lines** Fred Olsen House, White House Road, Ipswich, Suffolk IP1 5LL, tel: 01473 742424; <www.fredolsen.co.uk>. Three ships appealing to a mainly British market. Comfortable rather than the height of luxury and with a loyal following.

• **Hebridean Island Cruises** Griffin House, Broughton Hall, Skipton, North Yorkshire BD23 3AN, tel: 01756 704704; <www.

hebridean.co.uk>. Very small, deluxe ships sailing imaginative itineraries in Scotland and all over the Mediterranean.

• **Holland America Line (HAL)** UK: Carnival House, 5 Gainsford Street, London SE1 2NE, tel: 020 7940 4477; US: 300 Elliot Avenue West, Seattle, WA 98119, tel: 1-877 724 5425; <www. hollandamerica.com>. Subsidiary of Carnival Corporation. Large fleet of elegant ships appealing mainly to US citizens in the older age bracket. Some wonderfully adventurous itineraries in Europe.

• **Island Cruises** Olivier House, 18 Marine Parade, Brighton BN2 1TL, tel: 08707 500414; <www.islandcruises.com>. Large, informal ship sailing seven-night itineraries out of Palma, Mallorca.

• **Louis Cruise Lines** Chesterfield House, 385–7 Euston Road, London NW1 3AU, tel: 020 7383 2882; <www.louiscruises.com>. Budget cruise line running two- and three-night breaks from Cyprus.

• **Mediterranean Shipping Company (MSC)** UK: Suite 208, Walmar House, 296 Regent Street, London W1B 3AW, tel: 020 7637 2525; US: 6750 North Andrews Avenue, Fort Lauderdale, FL 33309; tel: 1-954 772 6262/1-800 666 9333; <www.msccruises. com>. Italian-owned cruise line. Lively, value-for-money ships appealing to all ages and nationalities.

• **Norwegian Cruise Line (NCL)** UK: 1 Derry Street, London W8 5NN, tel: 0845 6588010; <www.uk.ncl.com>. US: 7665 Corporate Center Drive, Miami, FL 33126, tel: 305-358 6670; <www. ncl.com>. Large, pioneer of Freestyle Cruising, with all ships offering an informal setting and a wide choice of dining options. Appeals mainly to US nationals, with a good mix of ages, including families.

• **Ocean Village** Richmond House, Terminus Terrace, Southampton SO14 3PN, tel: 0845 4567888; <www.oceanvillageholidays.co.uk>. Modern, funky ship aimed at younger cruisers, sailing seven-night itineraries out of Palma. A division of Carnival Plc.

• **Orient Lines** UK: 1 Derry Street, Kensington, London W8 5NN, tel: 0845 658 8050; US: 7665 Corporate Center Drive, Miami, FL

33126, tel: 0800 333-7300; <www.orientlines.com>. Cultural cruises aimed at an international market on the popular, elegant *Marco Polo*.

• **P&O Cruises** UK: Richmond House, Terminus Terrace, Southampton SO14 3PN, tel: 08453 555333; <www.pocruises. co.uk>; US: 24305 Town Center Drive, Santa Clarita, CA 91355-4999, tel: 800-252 0158 (California only) or 800-421 0522, 213-553 1770; <www.pocruises.com>. British sister company of Princess Cruises. Large, modern ships appealing to a mainly British market. Particularly suited to families.

• **Princess Cruises** UK: Richmond House, Terminus Terrace, Southampton SO14 3PN, tel: 08453 555800; <www.princesscruises. co.uk>; US: 24305 Town Center Drive, Santa Clarita, CA 91355-4999; <www.princesscruises.com>. Large, luxurious, modern ships with broad appeal.

• **Radisson Seven Seas Cruises** UK: Suites 3 and 4, Canute Chambers, Canute Road, Southampton SO14 3AB, tel: 02380 682280; <www.rssc.co.uk>; US: 600 Corporate Drive, Suite 410, Fort Lauderdale, FL 33334, tel: 800-477 7500; <www.rssc.com>.

• **Royal Caribbean International/Celebrity Cruises** UK: Royal Caribbean House, Addlestone Road, Weybridge, Surrey KT15 2UE, tel: 0800 018 2020 (Royal Caribbean) or 0800 018 2525 (for Celebrity Cruises); <www.royalcaribbean.co.uk>; US: 1050 Caribbean Way, Miami, FL 33132, tel: 800-722 5045 ext 50961 (for Royal Caribbean) and 800-852 7239 (for Celebrity); <www.royalcaribbean.com> and <www.celebritycruises.com>. Sister cruise lines, of which Celebrity is the more upmarket. Both operate a large, luxurious, modern fleet. RCI in particular appeals to families and has some very well-equipped ships sailing in Europe in the summer.

• **SeaDream Yacht Club** European office: Smalvollveien 65, PO Box 50, Bryn N-0611 Oslo, Norway tel: 47 23 28 96 60; US: 2601 South Bayshore Drive, Penthouse 1B, Coconut Grove, Florida 33133, tel: 800-707 4911 or 305-856 5622; <www.seadreamyachtclub.com>. 100-passenger luxury motor yachts; sophisticated but casual.

• **Silversea Cruises** UK: 77/79 Great Eastern Street, London EC2A 3HU, tel: 0870 333 7030; US: 110 East Broward Blvd, Fort Lauderdale, FL 33301, tel: 877-760 9052; <www.silversea.com>. The ultimate in luxury; four elegant, all-inclusive ships with international appeal.

• **Star Clippers** UK: Fred Olsen, Crown House, Crown Street, Ipswich, IP1 3HS, tel: 01473 292029; US: 7200 NW 19th Street, Suite 206, Miami, FL 33126, tel: 305-442 1611; <www.starclippers. com>. Romantic sailing cruises on elegant clipper ships. International appeal.

• **Swan Hellenic** UK: Richmond House, Terminus Terrace, Southampton SO14 3PN, tel: 08453 555111 or, from overseas, +44 (0)2380 683606; <www.swanhellenic.com>; US/Canada: 631 Commack Road, Suite 1A, Commack NY 11725, tel: 877-800 swan (toll-free) or 631-858 1263. Cultural cruises on board the elegant *Minerva II*, which roams the world and spends summer in Europe.

• **Thomson Cruises** Thomson Holidays, Greater London House, Hampstead Road, London NW1 7SD tel: 0870 550 2562; <www. thomson.co.uk>. Seven- and 14-night cruise-and-stay holidays in the Mediterranean on a fleet of popular and well-equipped ships.

• **Voyages of Discovery** Lynnem House, 1 Victoria Way, Burgess Hill, West Sussex RH15 9NF, tel: 01444 462150; <www.voyagesof discovery.com>. Affordable cultural cruising.

• **Windstar Cruises** UK: Carnival House, 5 Gainsford Street, London SE1 2NE, tel: 020 7940 4488; US: 300 Elliott Avenue West, Seattle, WA 98119, tel: 1-877 724 5425; <www.windstarcruises. com>. Luxurious large yachts, which travel partly under sail and have a very glamorous appeal. Popular with honeymooners.

• **Yachts of Seabourn** UK: Richmond House, Terminus Terrace, Southampton SO14 3PN, tel: 0845 070 0500; US: 6100 Blue Lagoon Drive, Suite 400, Miami, FL 33126, tel: 305-463 3000; <www.seabourn.com>. Elegant yacht-ships cruising small, chic Mediterranean islands and ports. All-inclusive and very upmarket.

INDEX